Marx
Joyce
Hardy
Abbott
Defoe
Austen
Melville
Machiavelli
Montaigne
Chesterton
Emerson
Cooper
Hugo
Eliot
Grimm
Haggard
Christie
Carroll
Molière
Stoker
Wilde
Byron
Schiller
Maupassant
Engels
Garnett
Fitzgerald
Einstein
Hawthorne
Smith
Kafka
Goethe
Dostoyevsky
Hall
Cotton
Kipling
Doyle
Willis
Baum
Henry
Nietzsche
Leslie
Dumas
Flaubert
Turgenev
Balzac
Stockton
Vatsyayana
Crane
Burroughs
Verne
Curtis
Tocqueville
Vinci
Homer
Gogol
Busch
Widger
Tolstoy
Whitman
Darwin
Thoreau
Twain
Potter
Scott
Plato
Harte
Freud
Zola
Lawrence
Kant
Jowett
Stevenson
Dickens
Burton
Hesse
Andersen
London
Descartes
Cervantes
Voltaire
Poe
Aristotle
Wells
Cooke
Hale
James
Hastings
Bunner
Shakespeare
Irving
Richter
Chambers
da
Shaw
Doré
Benedict
Alcott
Dante
Chekhov
Wodehouse
Pushkin
Swift
Newton

The Memoirs of General Philip H. Sheridan, Volume I., Part 2

Philip Henry Sheridan

Imprint

This book is part of TREDITION CLASSICS

Author: Philip Henry Sheridan
Cover design: Buchgut, Berlin – Germany

Publisher: tredition GmbH, Hamburg - Germany
ISBN: 978-3-8424-6009-6

www.tredition.com
www.tredition.de

PERSONAL MEMOIRS
OF
P. H. SHERIDAN

PERSONAL
MEMOIRS
OF
P.H.SHERIDAN

VOLUME
·II·

CHAS.L.WEBSTER
& Co.

PERSONAL
MEMOIRS
OF
P.H.SHERIDAN

VOLUME
·I·

CHAS.L.WEBSTER
& Co.

PERSONAL MEMOIRS

OF

P. H. SHERIDAN.

GENERAL UNITED STATES ARMY.

IN TWO VOLUMES

VOL. I.

NEW YORK:

CHARLES L. WEBSTER & COMPANY,

1888.

CONTENTS

ILLUSTRATIONS

Steel Portrait—General P. H. Sheridan
General Sheridan's War Horse "Rienzi"

MAPS

Northeastern Mississippi
Battle of Booneville
Map Showing the Field of Operations of the Army of the Cumber-
land
in 1862 and 1863
Battle—field of Stone River
Positions of General Sheridan's Division
in the Battle of Chickamauga

VOLUME I.

Part 2.

By Philip Henry Sheridan

CHAPTER IX.

EXPEDITION TO BOONEVILLE—DESTROYING SUPPLIES—CONFEDERATE STRAGGLERS—SUCCESS OF THE EXPEDITION—A RECONNOISSANCE—THE IMPORTANCE OF BODILY SUSTENANCE—THE BATTLE OF BOONEVILLE—RECOMMENDED FOR APPOINTMENT AS A BRIGADIER-GENERAL.

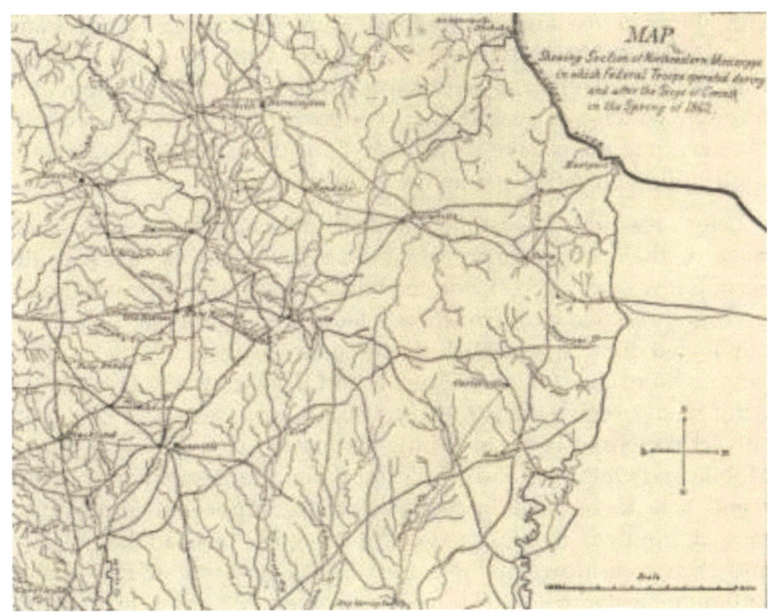

The expedition referred to by General Halleck in his parting conversation was composed of the Second Michigan and Second Iowa regiments of cavalry, formed into a brigade under command of Colonel Washington L. Elliott, of the Second Iowa. It was to start on the night of the 27th of May at 12 o'clock, and proceed by a circuitous route through Iuka, Miss., to Booneville, a station on the Mobile and Ohio Railroad, about twenty-two miles below Corinth, and accomplish all it could in the way of destroying the enemy's supplies and cutting his railroad communications.

The weather in that climate was already warm, guides unobtainable, and both men and horses suffered much discomfort from the heat, and fatigue from the many delays growing out of the fact that we were in almost total ignorance of the roads leading to the point that we desired to reach. In order that we might go light we carried only sugar, coffee, and salt, depending on the country for meat and bread. Both these articles were scarce, but I think we got all there was, for our advent was so unexpected by the people of the region through which we passed that, supposing us to be Confederate cavalry, they often gave us all they had, the women and servants contributing most freely from their, reserve stores.

Before reaching Booneville I had the advance, but just as we arrived on the outskirts of the town the brigade was formed with the Second Iowa on my right, and the whole force moved forward, right in front, preceded by skirmishers. Here we encountered the enemy, but forced him back with little resistance. When we had gained possession of the station, Colonel Elliott directed me to take the left wing of my regiment, pass to the south, and destroy a bridge or culvert supposed to be at a little distance below the town on the Mobile and Ohio Railroad. The right wing, or other half of the regiment, was to be held in reserve for my support if necessary. I moved rapidly in the designated direction till I reached the railroad, and then rode down it for a mile and a half, but found neither bridge nor culvert. I then learned that there was no bridge of any importance except the one at Baldwin, nine miles farther down, but as I was aware, from information recently received, that it was defended by three regiments and a battery, I concluded that I could best accomplish the purpose for which I had been detached—crippling the road—by tearing up the track, bending the rails, and burning the cross-ties. This was begun with alacrity at four different points, officers and men vieing with one another in the laborious work of destruction. We had but few tools, and as the difficulties to overcome were serious, our progress was slow, until some genius conceived the idea that the track, rails and ties, might be lifted from its bed bodily, turned over, and subjected to a high heat; a convenient supply of dry fence-rails would furnish ample fuel to render the rails useless. In this way a good deal of the track was effectively broken up, and communication by rail from Corinth to the south entirely cut off. While we were still busy in wrecking the road, a dash was made at my right and rear by a squadron of Confederate cavalry. This was handsomely met by the reserve under Captain Archibald P. Campbell, of the Second Michigan, who, dismounting a portion of his command, received the enemy with such a volley from his Colt's repeating rifles that the squadron broke and fled in all directions. We were not molested further, and resumed our work, intending to extend the break toward Baldwin, but receiving orders from Elliott to return to Booneville immediately, the men were recalled, and we started to rejoin the main command.

In returning to Booneville, I found the railroad track above where I had struck it blocked by trains that we had thus cut off, and the woods and fields around the town covered with several thousand Confederate soldiers. These were mostly convalescents and disheartened stragglers belonging to General Beauregard's army, and from them we learned that Corinth was being evacuated. I spent some little time in an endeavor to get these demoralized men into an open field, with a view to some future disposition of them; but in the midst of the undertaking I received another order from Colonel Elliott to join him at once. The news of the evacuation had also reached Elliott, and had disclosed a phase of the situation so different from that under which he had viewed it when we arrived at Booneville, that he had grown anxious to withdraw, lest we should be suddenly pounced upon by an overwhelming force from some one of the columns in retreat. Under such circumstances my prisoners would prove a decided embarrassment, so I abandoned further attempts to get them together—not even paroling them, which I thought might have been done with but little risk.

In the meantime the captured cars had been fired, and as their complete destruction was assured by explosions from those containing ammunition, they needed no further attention, so I withdrew my men and hastened to join Elliott, taking along some Confederate officers whom I had retained from among four or five hundred prisoners captured when making the original dash below the town.

The losses in my regiment, and, in fact, those of the entire command, were insignificant. The results of the expedition were important; the railroad being broken so thoroughly as to cut off all rolling stock north of Booneville, and to place at the service of General Halleck's army the cars and locomotives of which the retreating Confederates were now so much in need. In addition, we burned twenty-six cars containing ten thousand stand of small arms, three pieces of artillery, a great quantity of clothing, a heavy supply of ammunition, and the personal baggage of General Leonidas Polk. A large number of prisoners, mostly sick and convalescent, also fell into our hands; but as we could not carry them with us—such a hurried departure was an immediate necessity, by reason of our critical situation—the process of paroling them was not completed, and they doubtless passed back to active service in the Confederacy, properly enough unrecognized as prisoners of war by their superiors.

In returning, the column marched back by another indirect route to its old camp near Farmington, where we learned that the whole army had moved into and beyond Corinth, in pursuit of Beauregard, on the 13th of May, the very day we had captured Booneville. Although we had marched about one hundred and eighty miles in four days, we were required to take part, of course, in the pursuit of the Confederate army. So, resting but one night in our old camp, we were early in the saddle again on the morning of the 2d of June. Marching south through Corinth, we passed on the 4th of June the scene of our late raid, viewing with much satisfaction, as we took the road toward Blackland, the still smoldering embers of the burned trains.

On the 4th of June I was ordered to proceed with my regiment along the Blackland road to determine the strength of the enemy in that direction, as it was thought possible we might capture, by a concerted movement which General John Pope had suggested to General Halleck, a portion of Beauregard's rear guard. Pushing the Confederate scouts rapidly in with a running fire for a mile or more, while we were approaching a little stream, I hoped to gobble the main body of the enemy's pickets. I therefore directed the sabre battalion of the regiment, followed by that portion of it armed with revolving rifles, to dash forward in column, cut off these videttes before they could cross the stream, and then gather them in. The pickets fled hastily, however, and a pell-mell pursuit carried us over the stream at their heels by a little bridge, with no thought of halting till we gained a hill on the other side, and suddenly found ourselves almost in the camp of a strong body of artillery and infantry. Captain Campbell being in advance, hurriedly dismounted his battalion for a further forward movement on foot, but it was readily seen that the enemy was present in such heavy force as almost to ensure our destruction, and I gave orders for a hasty withdrawal. We withdrew without loss under cover of thick woods, aided much, however, by the consternation of the Confederates, who had hardly recovered from their surprise at our sudden appearance in their camp before we had again placed the stream between them and us by recrossing the bridge. The reconnoissance was a success in one way — that is, in finding out that the enemy was at the point supposed by, General Pope; but it also had a tendency to accelerate Beauregard's retreat, for in a day or two his whole line fell back as far south as Guntown, thus rendering abortive the plans for bagging a large portion of his army.

General Beauregard's evacuation of Corinth and retreat southward were accomplished in the face of a largely superior force of Union troops, and he reached the point where he intended to halt for reorganization without other loss than that sustained in the destruction of the cars and supplies at Booneville, and the capture of some stragglers and deserters that fell into our hands while we were pressing his rear from General Pope's flank. The number of these was quite large, and indicated that the enemy was considerably demoralized. Under such circumstances, an energetic and skillfully directed pursuit might not have made certain the enemy's destruction, but it would largely have aided in disintegrating his forces, and I never could quite understand why it was not ordered. The desultory affairs between rear and advance guards seemed as a general, thing to have no particular purpose in view beyond finding out where the enemy was, and when he was found, since no supporting colums were at hand and no one in supreme control was present to give directions, our skirmishing was of little avail and brought but small reward.

A short time subsequent to these occurrences, Colonel Elliott was made a brigadier-general, and as General Pope appointed him his Chief-of-Staff, I, on the 11th of June, 1862, fell in command of the brigade by seniority. For the rest of the month but little of moment occurred, and we settled down into camp at Booneville on the 26th of June, in a position which my brigade had been ordered to take up some twenty miles, in advance of the main army for the purpose of covering its front. Although but a few days had elapsed from the date of my appointment as colonel of the Second Michigan to that of my succeeding to the command of the brigade, I believe I can say with propriety that I had firmly established myself in the confidence of the officers and men of the regiment, and won their regard by thoughtful care. I had striven unceasingly to have them well fed and well clothed, had personally looked after the selection of their camps, and had maintained such a discipline as to allay former irritation.

Men who march, scout, and fight, and suffer all the hardships that fall to the lot of soldiers in the field, in order to do vigorous work must have the best bodily sustenance, and every comfort that can be provided. I knew from practical experience on the frontier that my efforts in this direction would not only be appreciated, but requited by personal affection and gratitude; and, further, that such exertions would bring the best results to me. Whenever my authority would permit I saved my command from needless sacrifices and unnecessary toil; therefore, when hard or daring work was to be done I expected the heartiest response, and always got it. Soldiers are averse to seeing their comrades killed without compensating results, and none realize more quickly than they the blundering that often takes place on the field of battle. They want some tangible indemnity for the loss of life, and as victory is an offset the value of which is manifest, it not only makes them content to shed their blood, but also furnishes evidence of capacity in those who command them. My regiment had lost very few men since coming under my command, but it seemed, in the eyes of all who belonged to it, that casualties to the enemy and some slight successes for us had repaid every sacrifice, and in consequence I had gained not only their confidence as soldiers, but also their esteem and love as men, and to a degree far beyond what I then realized.

As soon as the camp of my brigade was pitched at Booneville, I began to scout in every direction, to obtain a knowledge of the enemy's whereabouts and learn the ground about me. My standing in drawing at the Military Academy had never been so high as to warrant the belief that I could ever prove myself an expert, but a few practical lessons in that line were impressed on me there, and I had retained enough to enable me to make rough maps that could be readily understood, and which would be suitable to replace the erroneous skeleton outlines of northern Mississippi, with which at this time we were scantily furnished; so as soon as possible I compiled for the use of myself and my regimental commanders an information map of the surrounding country. This map exhibited such details as country roads, streams, farmhouses, fields, woods, and swamps, and such other topographical features as would be useful. I must confess that my crude sketch did not evidence much artistic merit, but it was an improvement on what we already possessed in the way of details to guide the command, and this was what I most needed; for it was of the first importance that in our exposed condition we should be equipped with a thorough knowledge of the section in which we were operating, so as to be prepared to encounter an enemy already indicating recovery from the disorganizing effects of his recent retreat.

In the immediate vicinity of Booneville the country was covered with heavy forests, with here and there clearings or intervening fields that had been devoted to the cultivation of cotton and corn. The ground was of a low character, typical of northeastern Mississippi, and abounded in small creeks that went almost totally dry even in short periods of drought, but became flooded with muddy water under the outpouring of rain peculiar to a semi-tropical climate. In such a region there were many chances of our being surprised, especially by an enemy who knew the country well, and whose ranks were filled with local guides; and great precautions as well as the fullest information were necessary to prevent disaster. I therefore endeavored to familiarize all with our surroundings, but scarcely had matters begun to shape themselves as I desired when our annihilation was attempted by a large force of Confederate cavalry.

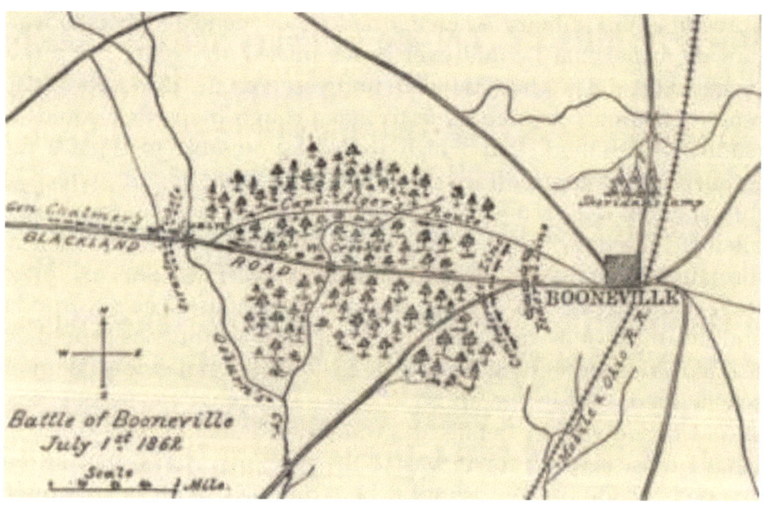

On the morning of July 1, 1862, a cavalry command of between five and six thousand-men, under the Confederate General James R. Chalmers, advanced on two roads converging near Booneville. The head of the enemy's column on the Blackland and Booneville road came in contact with my pickets three miles and a half west of Booneville. These pickets, under Lieutenant Leonidas S. Scranton, of the Second Michigan Cavalry, fell back slowly, taking advantage of every tree or other cover to fire from till they arrived at the point where the converging roads joined. At this junction there was a strong position in the protecting timber, and here Scranton made a firm stand, being reinforced presently by the few men he had out as pickets on the road to his left, a second company I had sent him from camp, and subsequently by three companies more, all now commanded by Captain Campbell. This force was dismounted and formed in line, and soon developed that the enemy was present in large numbers. Up to this time Chalmers had shown only the heads of his columns, and we had doubts as to his purpose, but now that our resistance forced him to deploy two regiments on the right and left of the road, it became apparent that he meant business, and that there was no time to lose in preparing to repel his attack.

Full information of the situation was immediately sent me, and I directed Campbell to hold fast, if possible, till I could support him, but if compelled to retire he was authorized to do so slowly, taking advantage of every means that fell in his way to prolong the fighting. Before this I had stationed one battalion of the Second Iowa in Booneville, but Colonel Edward Hatch, commanding that regiment, was now directed to leave one company for the protection of our camp a little to the north of the station, and take the balance of the Second Iowa, with the battalion in Booneville except two sabre companies, and form the whole in rear of Captain Campbell, to protect his flanks and support him by a charge should the enemy break his dismounted line.

While these preparations were being made, the Confederates attempted to drive Campbell from his position by a direct attack through an open field. In this they failed, however, for our men, reserving their fire until the enemy came within about thirty yards, then opened on him with such a shower of bullets from our Colt's rifles that it soon became too hot for him, and he was repulsed with considerable loss. Foiled in this move, Chalmers hesitated to attack again in front, but began overlapping both flanks of Campbell's line by force of numbers, compelling Campbell to retire toward a strong position I had selected in his rear for a line on which to make our main resistance. As soon as the enemy saw this withdrawing he again charged in front, but was again as gallantly repelled as in the first assault, although the encounter was for a short time so desperate as to have the character of a hand-to-hand conflict, several groups of friend and foe using on each other the butts of their guns.

At this juncture the timely arrival of Colonel Hatch with the Second Iowa gave a breathing-spell to Campbell, and made the Confederates so chary of further direct attacks that he was enabled to retire; and at the same time I found opportunity to make disposition of the reinforcement to the best advantage possible, placing the Second Iowa on the left of the new line and strengthening Campbell on its right with all the men available.

In view of his numbers, the enemy soon regained confidence in his ability to overcome us, and in a little while again began his flanking movements, his right passing around my left flank some distance, and approaching our camp and transportation, which I had forbidden to be moved out to the rear. Fearing that he would envelop us and capture the camp and transportation, I determined to take the offensive. Remembering a circuitous wood road that I had become familiar with while making the map heretofore mentioned, I concluded that the most effective plan would be to pass a small column around the enemy's left, by way of this road, and strike his rear by a mounted charge simultaneously with an advance of our main line on his front. I knew that the attack in rear would be a most hazardous undertaking, but in the face of such odds as the enemy had the condition of affairs was most critical, and could be relieved, only by a bold and radical change in our tactics; so I at once selected four sabre companies, two from the Second Michigan and two from the Second Iowa, and placing Captain Alger, of the former regiment, in command of them, I informed him that I expected of them the quick and desperate work that is usually imposed on a forlorn hope.

To carry out the purpose now in view, I instructed Captain Alger to follow the wood road as it led around the left of the enemy's advancing forces, to a point where 'it joined the Blackland road, about three miles from Booneville, and directed him, upon reaching the Blackland road, to turn up it immediately, and charge the rear of the enemy's line. Under no circumstances was he to deploy the battalion, but charge in column right through whatever he came upon, and report to me in front of Booneville, if at all possible for him to get there. If he failed to break through the enemy's line, he was to go ahead as far as he could, and then if any of his men were left, and he was able to retreat, he was to do so by the same route he had taken on his way out. To conduct him on this perilous service I sent along a thin, sallow, tawny-haired Mississippian named Beene, whom I had employed as a guide and scout a few days before, on account of his intimate knowledge of the roads, from the public thoroughfares down to the insignificant by-paths of the neighboring swamps. With such guidance I felt sure that the column would get to the desired point without delay, for there was no danger of its being lost or misled by taking any of the many by-roads which traversed the dense forests through which it would be obliged to pass. I also informed Alger that I should take the reserve and join the main line in front of Booneville for the purpose of making an advance of my whole force, and that as a signal he must have his men cheer loudly when he struck the enemy's rear, in order that my attack might be simultaneous with his.

I gave him one hour to go around and come back through the enemy, and when he started I moved to the front with the balance of the reserve, to put everything I had into the fight. This meant an inestimable advantage to the enemy in case of our defeat, but our own safety demanded the hazard. All along our attenuated line the fighting was now sharp, and the enemy's firing indicated such numerical strength that fear of disaster to Alger increased my anxiety terribly as the time set for his cheering arrived and no sound of it was heard.

Relying, however, on the fact that Beene's knowledge of the roads would prevent his being led astray, and confident of Alger's determination to accomplish the purpose for which he set out, as soon as the hour was up I ordered my whole line forward. Fortunately, just as this moment a locomotive and two cars loaded with grain for my horses ran into Booneville from Corinth. I say fortunately, because it was well known throughout the command that in the morning, when I first discovered the large numbers of the enemy, I had called for assistance; and my troops, now thinking that reinforcements had arrived by rail from Rienzi, where a division of infantry was encamped, and inspirated by this belief, advanced with renewed confidence and wild cheering. Meantime I had the engineer of the locomotive blow his whistle loudly, so that the enemy might also learn that a train had come; and from the fact that in a few moments he began to give way before our small force, I thought that this strategem had some effect. Soon his men broke, and ran in the utmost disorder over the country in every direction. I found later, however, that his precipitous retreat was due to the pressure on his left from the Second Iowa, in concert with the front attack of the Second Michigan, and the demoralization wrought in his rear by Alger, who had almost entirely accomplished the purpose of his expedition, though he had failed to come through, or so near that I could hear the signal agreed upon before leaving Booneville.

After Alger had reached and turned up the Blackland road, the first thing he came across was the Confederate headquarters; the officers and orderlies about which he captured and sent back some distance to a farm-house. Continuing on a gallop, he soon struck the rear of the enemy's line, but was unable to get through; nor did he get near enough for me to hear his cheering; but as he had made the distance he was to travel in the time allotted, his attack and mine were almost coincident, and the enemy, stampeded by the charges in front and rear, fled toward Blackland, with little or no attempt to capture Alger's command, which might readily have been done. Alger's troopers soon rejoined me at Booneville, minus many hats, having returned by their original route. They had sustained little loss except a few men wounded and a few temporarily missing. Among these was Alger himself, who was dragged from his saddle by the limb of a tree that, in the excitement of the charge, he was unable to flank. The missing had been dismounted in one way or another, and run over by the enemy in his flight; but they all turned up later, none the worse except for a few scratches and bruises.

My effective strength in this fight was 827 all told, and Alger's command comprised ninety officers and men. Chalmers's force was composed of six regiments and two battalions, and though I have been unable to find any returns from which to verify his actual numbers, yet, from the statements of prisoners and from information obtained from citizens along his line of march, it is safe to say that he had in the action not less than five-thousand men. Our casualties were not many—forty-one in all. His loss in killed and wounded was considerable, his most severely wounded—forty men—falling into our hands, having been left at farm-houses in the vicinity of the battlefield.

The victory in the face of such odds was most gratifying, and as it justified my disinclination—in fact, refusal—to retire from Booneville without fighting (for the purpose of saving my transportation, as directed by superior authority when I applied in the morning for reinforcements), it was to me particularly grateful. It was also very valuable in, view of the fact that it increased the confidence between the officers and men of my brigade and me, and gave us for the balance of the month not only comparative rest, but entire immunity from the dangers of a renewed effort to gobble my isolated outpost. In addition to all this, commendation from my immediate superiors was promptly tendered through oral and written congratulations; and their satisfaction at the result of the battle took definite form a few days later, in the following application for my promotion, when, by an expedition to Ripley, Miss., most valuable information as to the enemy's location and plans was captured:

"HEADQUARTERS ARMY OF THE MISSISSIPPI,
"JULY 30, 1862.—3.05 P. M.

"MAJOR-GENERAL HALLECK,
"Washington, D. C.

"Brigadiers scarce; good ones scarce. Asboth goes
on the month's leave you gave him ten months
since; Granger has temporary command. The un-
dersigned respectfully beg that you will obtain the
promotion of Sheridan. He is worth his weight in
gold. His Ripley expedition has brought us captured letters of immense value, as well as prisoners, showing the rebel plans and dispositions, as
you will learn from District Commander.

"W. S. ROSECRANS, Brigadier-General.
"C. C. SULLIVAN, " "
"G. GRANGER, " "
"W. L. ELLIOTT, " "
"A. ASBOTH, " " "

CHAPTER X.

IN CAMP NEAR RIENZI—GENERAL GRANGER—A VALUA-BLE CAPTURE AT RIPLEY—RAIDING A CORNFIELD—REPULSING AN ATTACK—PRESENTED WITH THE BLACK HORSE "RIENZI"—MEETING GENERAL GRANT—APPOINTED A BRIGADIER-GENERAL.

After the battle of Booneville, it was decided by General Rosecrans, on the advice of General Granger, that my position at Booneville was too much exposed, despite the fact that late on the evening of the fight my force had been increased by the addition of, a battery of four guns and two companies of infantry, and by the Third Michigan Cavalry, commanded by Colonel John K. Mizner; so I was directed to withdraw from my post and go into camp near Rienzi, Mississippi, where I could equally well cover the roads in front of the army, and also be near General Asboth's division of infantry, which occupied a line in rear of the town. This section of country, being higher and more rolling than that in the neighborhood of Booneville, had many advantages in the way of better camping-grounds, better grazing and the like, but I moved with reluctance, because I feared that my proximity to Asboth would diminish to a certain extent my independence of command.

General Asboth was a tall, spare, handsome man, with gray mustache and a fierce look. He was an educated soldier, of unquestioned courage, but the responsibilities of outpost duty bore rather heavily on him, and he kept all hands in a state of constant worry in anticipation of imaginary attacks. His ideas of discipline were not very rigid either, and as by this time there had been introduced into my brigade some better methods than those obtaining when it first fell to my command, I feared the effect should he, have any control over it, or meddle with its internal affairs. However, there was nothing to do but to move to the place designated, but General Granger, who still commanded the cavalry division to which the brigade belonged, so arranged matters with General Rosecrans, who had succeeded to the command of the Army of the Mississippi, that my independence was to be undisturbed, except in case of a general attack by the enemy.

We went into camp near Rienzi, July 22, sending back to the general field-hospital at Tuscumbia Springs all our sick — a considerable number — stricken down by the malarial influences around Booneville. In a few days the fine grazing and abundance of grain for our exhausted horses brought about their recuperation; and the many large open fields in the vicinity gave opportunity for drills and parades, which were much needed. I turned my attention to those disciplinary measures which, on account of active work in the field, had been necessarily neglected since the brigade had arrived at Pittsburg Landing, in April; and besides, we had been busy in collecting information by scouting parties and otherwise, in prosecution of the purpose for which we were covering the main army.

I kept up an almost daily correspondence with General Granger, concerning the, information obtained by scouts and reconnoitring parties, and he came often to Rienzi to see me in relation to this and other matters. Previously I had not had much personal association with Granger. While I was at Halleck's headquarters we met on one or two occasions, and the day I joined the Second Michigan at Farmington I saw him for a few moments, but, with such slight exception, our intercourse had been almost exclusively official. He had suggested my name, I was told, to Governor Blair, when the Governor was in search of an officer of the regular army to appoint to the colonelcy of the Second Michigan Cavalry, but his recommendation must have been mainly based on the favorable opinions he had heard expressed by General Halleck and by some of the officers of his staff, rather than from any personal knowledge of my capacity. Of course I was very grateful for this, but some of his characteristics did not impress me favorably, and I sometimes wished the distance between our camps greater. His most serious failing was an uncontrollable propensity to interfere with and direct the minor matters relating to the command, the details for which those under him were alone responsible. Ill-judged meddling in this respect often led to differences between us, only temporary it is true, but most harassing to the subordinate, since I was compelled by the circumstances of the situation not only invariably to yield my own judgment, but many a time had to play peacemaker — smoothing down ruffled feelings, that I knew had been excited by Granger's freaky and spasmodic efforts to correct personally some trifling fault that ought to have been left to a regimental or company commander to remedy. Yet with all these small blemishes Granger had many good qualities, and his big heart was so full of generous impulses and good motives as to far outbalance his short-comings; and notwithstanding the friction and occasional acerbity of our official intercourse, we maintained friendly relations till his death.

In pursuance of the fatal mistake made by dispersing Halleck's forces after the fall of Corinth, General Don Carlos Buell's Army of the Ohio had been started some time before on its march eastward toward Chattanooga; and as this movement would be followed of course by a manoeuvre on the part of the enemy, now at Tupelo under General Braxton Bragg, either to meet Buell or frustrate his designs by some counter-operation, I was expected to furnish, by scouting and all other means available, information as to what was going on within the Confederate lines. To do the work required, necessitated an increase of my command, and the Seventh Kansas Cavalry was therefore added to it, and my picket-line extended so as to cover from Jacinto southwesterly to a point midway between Rienzi and Booneville, and then northwesterly to the Hatchie River. Skirmishes between outposts on this line were of frequent occurrence, with small results to either side, but they were somewhat annoying, particularly in the direction of Ripley, where the enemy maintained a considerable outpost. Deciding to cripple if not capture this outpost, on the evening of July 27, I sent out an expedition under Colonel Hatch, which drove the enemy from the town of Ripley and took a few prisoners, but the most valuable prize was in the shape of a package of thirty-two private letters, the partial reading of which disclosed to me the positive transfer from Mississippi of most of Bragg's army, for the purpose of counteracting Buell's operations in northern Alabama and East Tennessee. This decisive evidence was of the utmost importance, and without taking time to read all the letters, I forwarded them to General Granger July 28, in a despatch which stated: "I deem it necessary to send them at once; the enemy is moving in large force on Chattanooga." Other than this the results of the expedition were few; and the enemy, having fled from Ripley with but slight resistance, accompanied by almost all the inhabitants, re-occupied the place next day after our people had quitted it, and resumed in due time his annoying attacks on our outposts, both sides trying to achieve something whenever occasion offered.

The prevalence of a severe drought had resulted in drying up many of the streams within the enemy's lines, and, in consequence, he was obliged to shift his camps often, and send his beef-cattle and mules near his outposts for water. My scouts kept me well posted in regard to the movements of both camps and herds; and a favorable opportunity presenting itself, I sent an expedition on August 14 to gather in some animals located on Twenty-Mile Creek, a stream always supplied with water from a source of never-failing, springs. Our side met with complete success in this instance, and when the expedition returned, we were all made happy by an abundance of fresh beef, and by some two hundred captured mules, that we thus added to our trains at a time when draft animals were much needed.

Rations for the men were now supplied in fair quantities, and the only thing required to make us wholly contented was plenty of grain for our animals. Because of the large number of troops then in West Tennessee and about Corinth, the indifferent railroad leading down from Columbus, Ky., was taxed to its utmost capacity to transport supplies. The quantity of grain received at Corinth from the north was therefore limited, and before reaching the different outposts, by passing through intermediate depots of supply, it had dwindled to insignificance. I had hopes, however, that this condition of things might be ameliorated before long by gathering a good supply of corn that was ripening in the neighborhood, and would soon, I thought, be sufficiently hard to feed to my animals. Not far from my headquarters there was a particularly fine field, which, with this end in view, I had carefully protected through the milky stage, to the evident disappointment of both Asboth's men and mine. They bore the prohibition well while it affected only themselves, but the trial was too great when it came to denying their horses; and men whose discipline kept faith with my guards during the roasting-ear period now fell from grace. Their horses were growing thin, and few could withstand the mute appeals of their suffering pets; so at night the corn, because of individual foraging, kept stealthily and steadily vanishing, until the field was soon fringed with only earless stalks. The disappearance was noticed, and the guard increased, but still the quantity of corn continued to grow less, the more honest troopers bemoaning the loss, and questioning the honor of those to whose safekeeping it had been entrusted. Finally, doubtless under the apprehension that through their irregularities the corn would all disappear and find its way to the horses in accordance with the stealthy enterprise of their owners, a general raid was made on the field in broad daylight, and though the guard drove off the marauders, I must admit that its efforts to keep them back were so unsuccessful that my hopes for an equal distribution of the crop were quickly blasted. One look at the field told that it had been swept clean of its grain. Of course a great row occurred as to who was to blame, and many arrests and trials took place, but there had been such an interchanging of cap numbers and other insignia that it was next to impossible to identify the guilty, and so much crimination and acrimony grew out of the affair that it was deemed best to drop the whole matter.

On August 27 about half of the command was absent reconnoitring, I having sent it south toward Tupelo, in the hope of obtaining some definite information regarding a movement to Holly Springs of the remainder of the Confederate army, under General Price, when about mid-day I was suddenly aroused by excited cries and sounds of firing, and I saw in a moment that the enemy was in my camp. He had come in on my right flank from the direction of the Hatchie River, pell-mell with our picket-post stationed about three miles out on the Ripley road. The whole force of the enemy comprised about eight hundred, but only his advance entered with my pickets, whom he had charged and badly stampeded, without, on their part, the pretense of a fight in behalf of those whom it was their duty to protect until proper dispositions for defense could be made. The day was excessively hot, one of those sultry debilitating days that had caused the suspending of all military exercises; and as most of the men were lounging or sleeping in their tents, we were literally caught napping. The alarm spread instantly through the camp, and in a moment the command turned out for action, somewhat in deshabille it is true, but none the less effective, for every man had grabbed his rifle and cartridge-box at the first alarm. Aided by a few shots from Captain Henry Hescock's battery, we soon drove the intruders from our camp in about the same disorder in which they had broken in on us. By this time Colonel Hatch and Colonel Albert L. Lee had mounted two battalions each, and I moved them out at a lively pace in pursuit, followed by a section of the battery. No halt was called till we came upon the enemy's main body, under Colonel Faulkner, drawn up in line of battle near Newland's store. Opening on him with the two pieces of artillery, I hurriedly formed line confronting him, and quickly and with but little resistance drove him in confusion from the field. The sudden turning of the tables dismayed Faulkner's men, and panic seizing them, they threw away every loose article of arms or clothing of which they could dismember themselves, and ran in the wildest disorder in a mad effort to escape. As the chase went on the panic increased, the clouds of dust from the road causing an intermingling of friend and foe. In a little while the affair grew most ludicrous, Faulkner's hatless and coatless men taking to the woods in such dispersed order and so demoralized that a good many prisoners were secured, and those of the enemy who escaped were hunted until dark. When the recall was sounded, our men came in loaded down with plunder in the shape of hats, haversacks, blankets, pistols, and shotguns, in a quantity which amply repaid for the surprise of the morning, but did not excuse the delinquent commander of our picket-guard, who a few days later was brought to a realizing sense of his duty by a court-martial.

Shortly after this affair Captain Archibald P. Campbell, of the Second Michigan Cavalry, presented me with the black horse called Rienzi, since made historical from having been ridden by me in many battles, conspicuously in the ride from Winchester to Cedar Creek, which has been celebrated in the poem by T. Buchanan Read. This horse was of Morgan stock, and then about three years old. He was jet black, excepting three white feet, sixteen hands high, and strongly built, with great powers of endurance. He was so active that he could cover with ease five miles an hour at his natural walking gait. The gelding had been ridden very seldom; in fact, Campbell had been unaccustomed to riding till the war broke out, and, I think, felt some disinclination to mount the fiery colt. Campbell had an affection for him, however, that never waned, and would often come to my headquarters to see his favorite, the colt being cared for there by the regimental farrier, an old man named John Ashley, who had taken him in charge when leaving Michigan, and had been his groom ever since. Seeing that I liked the horse—I had ridden him on several occasions—Campbell presented him to me on one of these visits, and from that time till the close of the war I rode him almost continuously, in every campaign and battle in which I took part, without once finding him overcome by fatigue, though on many occasions his strength was severely tested by long marches and short rations. I never observed in him any vicious habit; a nervousness and restlessness and switch of the tail, when everything about him was in repose, being the only indication that he might be untrustworthy. No one but a novice could be deceived by this, however, for the intelligence evinced in every feature, and his thoroughbred appearance, were so striking that any person accustomed to horses could not misunderstand such a noble animal. But Campbell thought otherwise, at least when the horse was to a certain degree yet untrained, and could not be pursuaded to ride him; indeed, for more than a year after he was given to me, Campbell still retained suspicions of his viciousness, though, along with this mistrust, an undiminished affection. Although he was several times wounded, this horse escaped death in action; and living to a ripe old age, died in 1878, attended to the last with all the care and surrounded with every comfort due the faithful service he had rendered.

In moving from Corinth east toward Chattanooga, General Buell's army was much delayed by the requirement that he should repair the Memphis and Charleston railroad as he progressed. The work of repair obliged him to march very slowly, and was of but little use when done, for guerrillas and other bands of Confederates destroyed the road again as soon as he had passed on. But worst of all, the time thus consumed gave General Bragg the opportunity to reorganize and increase his army to such an extent that he was able to contest the possession of Middle Tennessee and Kentucky. Consequently, the movement of this army through Tennessee and Kentucky toward the Ohio River—its objective points being Louisville and Cincinnati—was now well defined, and had already rendered abortive General Buell's designs on Chattanooga and East Tennessee. Therefore extraordinary efforts on the part of the Government became necessary, and the concentration of National troops at Louisville and Cincinnati to meet the contingency of Bragg's reaching those points was an obvious requirement. These troops were drawn from all sections in the West where it was thought they could be spared, and among others I was ordered to conduct thither—to Louisville or Cincinnati, as subsequent developments might demand—my regiment, Hescock's battery, the Second and Fifteenth Missouri, and the Thirty-sixth and Forty-fourth Illinois regiments of infantry, known as the "Pea Ridge Brigade." With this column I marched back to Corinth on the 6th of September, 1862, for the purpose of getting railroad transportation to Columbus, Kentucky.

At Corinth I met General Grant, who by this time had been reestablished in favor and command somewhat, General Halleck having departed for Washington to assume command of the army as General-in-Chief. Before and during the activity which followed his reinstatement, General Grant had become familiar with my services through the transmission to Washington of information I had furnished concerning the enemy's movements, and by reading reports of my fights and skirmishes in front, and he was loth to let me go. Indeed, he expressed surprise at seeing me in Corinth, and said he had not expected me to go; he also plainly showed that he was much hurt at the inconsiderate way in which his command was being depleted. Since I was of the opinion that the chief field of usefulness and opportunity was opening up in Kentucky, I did not wish him to retain me, which he might have done, and I impressed him with my conviction, somewhat emphatically, I fear. Our conversation ended with my wish gratified. I afterward learned that General Granger, whom General Grant did not fancy, had suggested that I should take to Cincinnati the main portion of Granger's command—the Pea Ridge Brigade—as well as the Second Michigan Cavalry, of which I was still colonel. We started that night, going by rail over the Mobile and Ohio road to Columbus, Ky., where we embarked on steamboats awaiting us. These boats were five in number, and making one of them my flag-ship, expecting that we might come upon certain batteries reported to be located upon the Kentucky shore of the Ohio, I directed the rest to follow my lead. Just before reaching Caseyville, the captain of a tin-clad gunboat that was patrolling the river brought me the information that the enemy was in strong force at Caseyville, and expressed a fear that my fleet could not pass his batteries. Accepting the information as correct, I concluded to capture the place before trying to pass up the river. Pushing in to the bank as we neared the town, I got the troops ashore and moved on Caseyville, in the expectation of a bloody fight, but was agreeably surprised upon reaching the outskirts of the village by an outpouring of its inhabitants—men, women, and children—carrying the Stars and Stripes, and making the most loyal professions. Similar demonstrations of loyalty had been made to the panic-stricken captain of the gunboat when he passed down the river, but he did not stay to ascertain their character, neither by landing nor by inquiry, for he assumed that on the Kentucky bank of the river there could be no loyalty. The result mortified the captain intensely; and deeming his convoy of little further use, he steamed toward Cairo in quest of other imaginary batteries, while I re-embarked at Caseyville, and continued up the Ohio undisturbed. About three miles below Cincinnati I received instructions to halt, and next day I was ordered by Major-General H. G. Wright to take my troops back to Louisville, and there assume command of the Pea Ridge Brigade, composed of the Second and Fifteenth Missouri, Thirty-sixth and Forty-fourth Illinois infantry, and of such other regiments as might be sent me in advance of the arrival of General Buell's army. When I reached Louisville I reported to Major-General William Nelson, who was sick, and who received me as he lay in bed. He asked me why I did not wear the shoulder-straps of my rank. I answered that I was the colonel of the Second Michigan cavalry, and had on my appropriate shoulder-straps. He replied that I was a brigadier-general for the Booneville fight, July 1, and that I should wear the shoulder-straps of that grade. I returned to my command and put it in camp; and as I had no reluctance to wearing the shoulder-straps of a brigadier-general, I was not long in procuring a pair, particularly as I was fortified next day by receiving from Washington official information of my appointment as a brigadier-general, to date from July 1, 1862, the day of the battle of Booneville

CHAPTER XI.

GOOD ADVICE FROM GENERAL NELSON—HIS TRAGIC DEATH—PUTTING LOUISVILLE IN A STATE OF DEFENSE—ASSIGNED TO THE COMMAND OF THE ELEVENTH DIVISION—CAPTURE OF CHAPLIN HEIGHTS—BATTLE OF PERRYVILLE—REPORTED AMONG THE KILLED—A THRILLING INCIDENT—GENERAL BUELL RELIEVED BY GENERAL ROSECRANS.

I reported to Major-General Nelson at the Galt House in Louisville, September 14, 1862, who greeted me in the bluff and hearty fashion of a sailor—for he had been in the navy till the breaking out of the war. The new responsibilities that were now to fall upon me by virtue of increased rank caused in my mind an uneasiness which, I think, Nelson observed at the interview, and he allayed it by giving me much good advice, and most valuable information in regard to affairs in Kentucky, telling me also that he intended I should retain in my command the Pea Ridge Brigade and Hescock's battery. This latter assurance relieved me greatly, for I feared the loss of these troops in the general redistribution which I knew must soon take place; and being familiar with their valuable service in Missouri, and having brought them up from Mississippi, I hoped they would continue with me. He directed me to take position just below the city with the Pea Ridge Brigade, Hescock's battery, and the Second Michigan Cavalry, informing me, at the same time, that some of the new regiments, then arriving under a recent call of the President for volunteers, would also be assigned to my command. Shortly after the interview eight new regiments and an additional battery joined me, thus making good his promise of more troops.

A few days later came Nelson's tragic end, shocking the whole country. Those of us in camp outside of the city were startled on the morning of September 29 by the news that General Jefferson C. Davis, of the Union Army, had shot General Nelson at the Galt House, and the wildest rumors in regard to the occurrence came thick and fast; one to the effect that Nelson was dead, another having it that he was living and had killed Davis, and still others reflecting on the loyalty of both, it being supposed by the general public at first that the difficulty between the two men had grown out of some political rather than official or personal differences. When the news came, I rode into the city to the Galt House to learn the particulars, reaching there about 10 o'clock in the forenoon. Here I learned that Nelson had been shot by Davis about two hours before, at the foot of the main stairway leading from the corridor just beyond the office to the second floor, and that Nelson was already dead. It was almost as difficult to get reliable particulars of the matter at the hotel as it had been in my camp, but I gathered that the two men had met first at an early hour near the counter of the hotel office, and that an altercation which had begun several days before in relation to something official was renewed by Davis, who, attempting to speak to Nelson in regard to the subject-matter of their previous dispute, was met by an insulting refusal to listen. It now appears that when Nelson made this offensive remark, Davis threw a small paper ball that he was nervously rolling between his fingers into Nelson's face, and that this insult was returned by Nelson slapping Davis (Killed by a Brother Soldier.—Gen. J. B. Fry.) in the face. But at the time, exactly what had taken place just before the shooting was shrouded in mystery by a hundred conflicting stories, the principal and most credited of which was that Davis had demanded from Nelson an apology for language used in the original altercation, and that Nelson's refusal was accompanied by a slap in the face, at the same moment denouncing Davis as a coward. However this may be, Nelson, after slapping Davis, moved toward the corridor, from which a stairway led to the second floor, and just as he was about to ascend, Davis fired with a pistol that he had obtained from some one near by after the blow had been struck. The ball entered Nelson's breast just above the heart, but his great strength enabled him to ascend the stairway notwithstanding the mortal character of the wound, and he did not fall till he reached the corridor on the second floor. He died about half an hour later. The tragedy cast a deep gloom over all who knew the men, for they both had many warm personal friends; and affairs at Louisville had hardly recovered as yet from the confused and discouraging condition which preceded the arrival of General Buell's army. General Buell reported the killing of Nelson to the authorities at Washington, and recommended the trial of Davis by court-martial, but no proceedings were ever instituted against him in either a civil or military court, so to this day it has not been determined judicially who was the aggressor. Some months later Davis was assigned to the command of a division in Buell's army after that officer had been relieved from its command.

Two Confederate armies, under General Kirby Smith and General Braxton Bragg, had penetrated into Kentucky, the one under Smith by the way of Cumberland Gap, the other and main army under Bragg by way of the Sequatche Valley, Glasgow, and Mumfordsville. Glasgow was captured by the enemy on the 17th of September, and as the expectation was that Buell would reach the place in time to save the town, its loss created considerable alarm in the North, for fears were now entertained that Bragg would strike Louisville and capture the city before Buell could arrive on the ground. It became necessary therefore to put Louisville in a state of defense, and after the cordon of principal works had been indicated, my troops threw up in one night a heavy line of rifle-pits south of the city, from the Bardstown pike to the river. The apprehended attack by Bragg never came, however, for in the race that was then going on between him and Buell on parallel roads, the Army of the Ohio outmarched the Confederates, its advance arriving at Louisville September 25.

General Buell immediately set about reorganizing the whole force, and on September 29 issued an order designating the troops under my command as the Eleventh Division, Army of the Ohio, and assigning Brigadier-General J. T. Boyle to command the division, and me to command one of its brigades. To this I could not object, of course, for I was a brigadier-general of very recent date, and could hardly expect more than a brigade. I had learned, however, that at least one officer to whom a high command had been given — a corps — had not yet been appointed a general officer by the President, and I considered it somewhat unfair that I should be relegated to a brigade, while men who held no commissions at all were being made chiefs of corps and divisions; so I sought an interview with General Buell's chief-of-staff, Colonel Fry, and, while not questioning Buell's good intentions nor his pure motives, insisted that my rights in the matter should be recognized. That same evening I was assigned to the command of the Eleventh Division, and began preparing it at once for a forward movement, which I knew must soon take place in the resumption of offensive operations by the Army of the Ohio.

During the interval from September 25 till October 1 there was among the officers much criticism of General Buell's management of the recent campaign, which had resulted in his retirement to Louisville; and he was particularly censured by many for not offering battle to General Bragg while the two armies were marching parallel to each other, and so near that an engagement could have been brought on at any one of several points—notably so at Glasgow, Kentucky, if there had been a desire to join issue. It was asserted, and by many conceded, that General Buell had a sufficient force to risk a fight. He was much blamed for the loss of Mumfordsville also. The capture of this point, with its garrison, gave Bragg an advantage in the race toward the Ohio River, which odds would most likely have ensured the fall of Louisville had they been used with the same energy and skill that the Confederate commander displayed from Chattanooga to Glasgow; but something always diverted General Bragg at the supreme moment, and he failed to utilize the chances falling to him at this time, for, deflecting his march to the north toward Bardstown, he left open to Buell the direct road to Louisville by way of Elizabethtown.

At Bardstown Bragg's army was halted while he endeavored to establish a Confederate government in Kentucky by arranging for the installation of a provisional governor at Lexington. Bragg had been assured that the presence of a Confederate army in Kentucky would so encourage the secession element that the whole State could be forced into the rebellion and his army thereby largely increased; but he had been considerably misled, for he now found that though much latent sympathy existed for his cause, yet as far as giving active aid was concerned, the enthusiasm exhibited by the secessionists of Kentucky in the first year of the war was now replaced by apathy, or at best by lukewarmness. So the time thus spent in political machinations was wholly lost to Bragg; and so little reinforcement was added to his army that it may be said that the recruits gained were not enough to supply the deficiencies resulting from the recent toilsome marches of the campaign.

In the meanwhile Buell had arrived at Louisville, system had been substituted for the chaos which had previously obtained there, and orders were issued for an advance upon the enemy with the purpose of attacking and the hope of destroying him within the limits of the "blue grass" region, and, failing in that, to drive him from Kentucky. The army moved October 1, 1862, and my division, now a part of the Third Corps, commanded by General C. C. Gilbert, marched directly on Bardstown, where it was thought the enemy would make a stand, but Bragg's troops retreated toward Perryville, only resisting sufficiently to enable the forces of General Kirby Smith to be drawn in closer—they having begun a concentration at Frankfort—so they could be used in a combined attack on Louisville as soon as the Confederate commander's political projects were perfected.

Much time was consumed by Buell's army in its march on Perryville, but we finally neared it on the evening of October 7. During the day, Brigadier-General Robert B. Mitchell's division of Gilbert's corps was in the advance on the Springfield pike, but as the enemy developed that he was in strong force on the opposite side of a small stream called Doctor's Creek, a tributary of Chaplin River, my division was brought up and passed to the front. It was very difficult to obtain water in this section of Kentucky, as a drought had prevailed for many weeks, and the troops were suffering so for water that it became absolutely necessary that we should gain possession of Doctor's Creek in order to relieve their distress. Consequently General Gilbert, during the night, directed me to push beyond Doctor's Creek early the next morning. At daylight on the 8th I moved out Colonel Dan McCook's brigade and Barnett's battery for the purpose, but after we had crossed the creek with some slight skirmishing, I found that we could not hold the ground unless we carried and occupied a range of hills, called Chaplin Heights, in front of Chaplin River. As this would project my command in the direction of Perryville considerably beyond the troops that were on either flank, I brought up Laiboldt's brigade and Hescock's battery to strengthen Colonel McCook. Putting both brigades into line we quickly carried the Heights, much to the surprise of the enemy, I think, for he did not hold on to the valuable ground as strongly as he should have done. This success not only ensured us a good supply of water, but also, later in the day, had an important bearing in the battle of Perryville. After taking the Heights, I brought up the rest of my division and intrenched, without much difficulty, by throwing up a strong line of rifle-pits, although the enemy's sharp-shooters annoyed us enough to make me order Laiboldt's brigade to drive them in on the main body. This was successfully done in a few minutes, but in pushing them back to Chaplin River, we discovered the Confederates forming a line of battle on the opposite bank, with the apparent purpose of an attack in force, so I withdrew the brigade to our intrenchments on the crest and there awaited the assault.

While this skirmishing was going on, General Gilbert—the corps commander—whose headquarters were located on a hill about a mile distant to the rear, kept sending me messages by signal not to bring on an engagement. I replied to each message that I was not bringing on an engagement, but that the enemy evidently intended to do so, and that I believed I should shortly be attacked. Soon after returning to the crest and getting snugly fixed in the rifle-pits, my attention was called to our left, the high ground we occupied affording me in that direction an unobstructed view. I then saw General A. McD. McCook's corps—the First-advancing toward Chaplin River by the Mackville road, apparently unconscious that the Confederates were present in force behind the stream. I tried by the use of signal flags to get information of the situation to these troops, but my efforts failed, and the leading regiments seemed to approach the river indifferently prepared to meet the sudden attack that speedily followed, delivered as it was from the chosen position of the enemy. The fury of the Confederate assault soon halted this advance force, and in a short time threw it into confusion, pushed it back a considerable distance, and ultimately inflicted upon it such loss of men and guns as to seriously cripple McCook's corps, and prevent for the whole day further offensive movement on his part, though he stoutly resisted the enemy's assaults until 4 o'clock in the afternoon.

Seeing McCook so fiercely attacked, in order to aid him I advanced Hescock's battery, supported by six regiments, to a very good position in front of a belt of timber on my extreme left, where an enfilading fire could be opened on that portion of the enemy attacking the right of the First Corps, and also on his batteries across

Chaplin River. But at this juncture he placed two batteries on my right and began to mass troops behind them, and General Gilbert, fearing that my intrenched position on the heights might be carried, directed me to withdraw Hescock and his supports and return them to the pits. My recall was opportune, for I had no sooner got back to my original line than the Confederates attacked me furiously, advancing almost to my intrenchments, notwithstanding that a large part of the ground over which they had to move was swept by a heavy fire of canister from both my batteries. Before they had quite reached us, however, our telling fire made them recoil, and as they fell back, I directed an advance of my whole division, bringing up my reserve regiments to occupy the crest of the hills; Colonel William P. Carlin's brigade of Mitchell's division meanwhile moving forward on my right to cover that flank. This advance pressed the enemy to Perryville, but he retired in such good order that we gained nothing but some favorable ground that enabled me to establish my batteries in positions where they could again turn their attention to the Confederates in front of McCook, whose critical condition was shortly after relieved, however, by a united pressure of Gilbert's corps against the flank of McCook's assailants, compelling them to retire behind Chaplin River.

The battle virtually ended about 4 o'clock in the afternoon, though more or less desultory firing continued until dark. Considering the severity of the engagement on McCook's front, and the reverses that had befallen him, I question if, from that part of the line, much could have been done toward retrieving the blunders of the day, but it did seem to me that, had the commander of the army been able to be present on the field, he could have taken advantage of Bragg's final repulse, and there would have remained in our hands more than the barren field. But no attempt was made to do anything more till next morning, and then we secured little except the enemy's killed and most severely wounded.

The operations of my division during the engagement pleased. General Gilbert very much, and he informed me that he would relax a rigidly enforced order which General Buell had issued some days before, sufficiently to permit my trains to come to the front and supply my almost starving troops with rations. The order in question was one of those issued, doubtless with a good intent, to secure generally the safety of our trains, but General Gilbert was not elastic, and on the march he had construed the order so illiberally that it was next to impossible to supply the men with food, and they were particularly short in this respect on the eve of the battle. I had then endeavored to persuade him to modify his iron-clad interpretation of the order, but without effect, and the only wagons we could bring up from the general parks in rear were ambulances and those containing ammunition. So to gain access to our trains was a great boon, and at that moment a more welcome result than would have been a complete victory minus this concession.

When the battle ceased General Gilbert asked me to join him at Buell's headquarters, which were a considerable distance to the rear, so after making some dispositions for the evening I proceeded there as requested. I arrived just as Buell was about to sit down to his supper, and noticing that he was lame, then learned that he had been severely injured by a recent fall from his horse. He kindly invited me to join him at the table, an invitation which I accepted with alacrity, enjoying the meal with a relish known only to a very-hungry man, for I had eaten nothing since morning. Of course the events of the day were the chief topic of discussion—as they were during my stay at headquarters—but the conversation indicated that what had occurred was not fully realized, and I returned to my troops impressed with the belief that General Buell and his staff-officers were unconscious of the magnitude of the battle that had just been fought.

It had been expected by Buell that he would fight the enemy on the 9th of October, but the Confederates disposed of that proposition by attacking us on the 8th, thus disarranging a tactical conception which, with our superior numbers, would doubtless have proved successful had it not been anticipated by an enterprising foe. During the battle on the 8th the Second Corps, under General Thomas L. Crittenden, accompanied by General George H. Thomas, lay idle the whole day for want of orders, although it was near enough to the field to take an active part in the fight; and, moreover, a large part of Gilbert's corps was unengaged during the pressure on McCook. Had these troops been put in on the enemy's left at any time after he assaulted McCook, success would have been beyond question; but there was no one on the ground authorized to take advantage of the situation, and the battle of Perryville remains in history an example of lost opportunities. This was due in some measure probably to General Buell's accident, but is mainly attributable to the fact that he did not clearly apprehend Bragg's aim, which was to gain time to withdraw behind Dick's River all the troops he had in Kentucky, for the Confederate general had no idea of risking the fate of his army on one general battle at a place or on a day to be chosen by the Union commander.

Considering the number of troops actually engaged, the losses to Buell were severe, amounting to something over five thousand in killed, wounded, and missing. Among the killed were two brigade commanders of much promise—General James S. Jackson and General William R. Terrill. McCook's corps lost twelve guns, some of which were recovered next day. The enemy's loss in killed and wounded we never learned, but it must have equalled ours; and about four thousand prisoners, consisting principally of sick and wounded, fell into our hands. In the first report of the battle sent North to the newspapers I was reported among the killed; but I was pleased to notice, when the papers reached us a few days later, that the error had been corrected before my obituary could be written.

The enemy retired from our front the night of the 8th, falling back on Harrodsburg to form a junction with Kirby Smith, and by taking this line of retreat opened to us the road to Danville and the chance for a direct march against his depot of supplies at Bryantsville. We did not take advantage of this opening, however, and late in the day—on the 9th—my division marched in pursuit, in the direction of Harrodsburg, which was the apex of a triangle having for its base a line from Perryville to Danville. The pursuit was slow, very slow, consuming the evening of the 9th and all of the 10th and 11th. By cutting across the triangle spoken of above, just south of the apex, I struck the Harrodsburg-Danville road, near Cave Springs, joining there Gilbert's left division, which had preceded me and marched through Harrodsburg. Here we again rested until the intention of the enemy could be divined, and we could learn on which side of Dick's River he would give us battle. A reconnoissance sent toward the Dickville crossing developed to a certainty that we should not have another engagement, however; for it disclosed the fact that Bragg's army had disappeared toward Camp Dick Robinson, leaving only a small rear-guard at Danville, which in turn quickly fled in the direction of Lancaster, after exchanging a few shots with Hescock's battery.

While this parting salute of deadly projectiles was going on, a little, daughter of Colonel William J. Landram, whose home was in Danville, came running out from his house and planted a small national flag on one of Hescock's guns. The patriotic act was so brave and touching that it thrilled all who witnessed the scene; and until the close of the war, when peace separated the surviving officers and men of the battery, that little flag was protected and cherished as a memento of the Perryville campaign.

Pursuit of the enemy was not continued in force beyond Crab Orchard, but some portions of the army kept at Bragg's heels until he crossed the Cumberland River, a part of his troops retiring to Tennessee by way of Cumberland Gap, but the major portion through Somerset. As the retreat of Bragg transferred the theatre of operations back to Tennessee, orders were now issued for a concentration of Buell's army at Bowling Green, with a view to marching it to Nashville, and my division moved to that point without noteworthy incident. I reached Bowling Green with a force much reduced by the losses sustained in the battle of Perryville and by sickness. I had started from Louisville on October 1 with twelve regiments of infantry—four old and eight new ones—and two batteries, but many poor fellows, overcome by fatigue, and diseases induced by the heat, dust, and drought of the season, had to be left at roadside hospitals. This was particularly the case with the new regiments, the men of which, much depressed by homesickness, and not yet inured to campaigning, fell easy victims to the hardships of war.

At Bowling Green General Buell was relieved, General W. S. Rosecrans succeeding him. The army as a whole did not manifest much regret at the change of commanders, for the campaign from Louisville on was looked upon generally as a lamentable failure, yet there were many who still had the utmost confidence in General Buell, and they repelled with some asperity the reflections cast upon him by his critics. These admirers held him blameless throughout for the blunders of the campaign, but the greater number laid every error at his door, and even went to the absurdity of challenging his loyalty in a mild way, but they particularly charged incompetency at Perryville, where McCook's corps was so badly crippled while nearly 30,000 Union troops were idle on the field, or within striking distance. With these it was no use to argue that Buell's accident stood in the way of his activity, nor that he did not know that the action had assumed the proportions of a battle. The physical disability was denied or contested, but even granting this, his detractors claimed that it did not excuse his ignorance of the true condition of the fight, and finally worsted his champions by pointing out that Bragg's retreat by way of Harrodsburg beyond Dick's River so jeopardized the Confederate army, that had a skillful and energetic advance of the Union troops been made, instead of wasting precious time in slow and unnecessary tactical manoeuvres, the enemy could have been destroyed before he could quit the State of Kentucky.

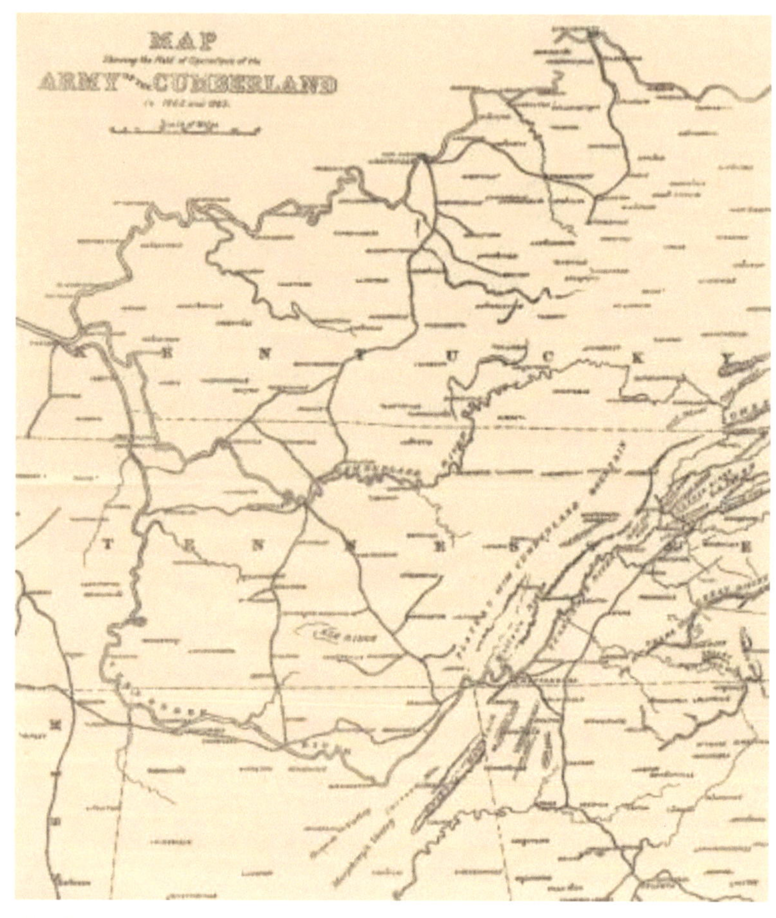

Enlarge

CHAPTER XII.

My division had moved from Crab Orchard to Bowling Green by easy marches, reaching this place November 1. General Rosecrans assumed command of the department October 30, at Louisville, and joined the army November 2. There had been much pressure brought to bear on General Buell to induce him to take measures looking to the occupancy of East Tennessee, and the clamor to this end from Washington still continued; but now that Bragg was south of the Cumberland River, in a position threatening Nashville, which was garrisoned by but a small force, it was apparent to every one at all conversant with the situation that a battle would have to be fought somewhere in Middle Tennessee. So, notwithstanding the pressure from Washington, the army was soon put in motion for Nashville, and when we arrived there my division went into camp north of the river, on a plateau just outside the little town of Edgefield, until the movements of the enemy should be further developed.

While in this camp, on the plantation of Mr. Hobson, there came to my headquarters one morning an East Tennessean named James Card, who offered to the Union cause his services in any capacity in which they might be made useful. This offer, and the relation of his personal history, were given with such sincerity of speech and manner that in a short time I became convinced of his honesty of purpose. He was a small, active, busy man, with a determined way about him, and his countenance indicated great intelligence. He gave minute information that was of inestimable value to me regarding East and Middle Tennessee and northern Georgia, for, with a view to the army's future movements, I was then making a study of the topography of this region, and posting myself as to Middle Tennessee, for all knew this would be the scene of active operations whenever the campaign was resumed. This man, like most of the

East Tennesseans whom I had met, was intensely loyal and patriotic, and the interview led in a few days to his employment as a scout and guide, and subsequently to the engaging in the same capacity of two of his brothers, who were good men; but not quite as active nor so intelligent as he was. Card had been a colporter, having pedled books, especially religious tracts, over all Middle and East Tennessee and Georgia, assisted by his brothers at times, and was therefore thoroughly familiar with these regions, their roads and inhabitants. He also preached to country congregations occasionally, when ministers were scarce, and I have no doubt often performed the functions of family physician in the mountain district. Thus his opportunities were great; and the loyal people in every section of the country being well known to him and his brothers, the three began, at this time, a system of scouting and investigation which bore its first-fruits in specifically locating the different divisions of Bragg's army, with statements of their strength and condition, and all with so much accuracy that I thereafter felt reasonably sure that I could at all times procure such knowledge of the enemy's operations as would well equip me for any contingency that might arise.

By the middle of November the enemy, having assembled his forces in Middle Tennessee, showed considerable boldness, and it became necessary to rearrange the Union lines; so my troops were moved to the south side of the river, out on the Murfreesboro' pike, to Mill Creek, distant from Nashville about seven miles. While we were in camp on Mill Creek the army was reorganized, and General Joshua W. Sill, at his own request, was assigned to my division, and took command of Colonel Nicholas Greusel's brigade. My division became at the same time the Third Division, Right Wing, Fourteenth Army Corps, its three brigades of four regiments each being respectively commanded by General Sill, Colonel Frederick Schaefer and Colonel Dan McCook; but a few days later Colonel George W. Roberts's brigade, from the garrison at Nashville, was substituted for McCook's.

General Sill was a classmate of mine at the Military Academy, having graduated in 1853. On graduating he was appointed to the Ordnance Corps, and served in that department at various arsenals and ordnance depots throughout the country till early in 1861, when he resigned to accept a professorship of mathematics and civil engineering at the Brooklyn Collegiate and Polytechnic Institute. At the breaking out of the war he immediately tendered his services to the Government, and soon rose to the colonelcy of the Thirty-Third Ohio Volunteers, and afterward to the rank of brigadier-general. I knew him well, and was glad that he came to my division, though I was very loth to relieve Colonel Greusel, of the Thirty-Sixth Illinois, who had already indicated much military skill and bravery, and at the battle of Perryville had handled his men with the experience of a veteran. Sill's modesty and courage were exceeded only by a capacity that had already been demonstrated in many practical ways, and his untimely death, almost within a month of his joining me, abruptly closed a career which, had it been prolonged a little more, not only would have shed additional lustre on his name, but would have been of marked benefit to his country.

Colonel Schaefer, of the Second Missouri Infantry, had been absent on sick-leave during the Kentucky campaign, but about this date he returned to duty, and by seniority fell in command of the second brigade. He was of German birth, having come from Baden, where, prior to 1848, he had been a non-commissioned officer in the service of his State. He took part as an insurgent in the so-called revolution which occurred at Baden in that year, and, compelled to emigrate on the suppression of the insurrection, made his way to this country and settled in St. Louis. Here the breaking out of the war found him, and through the personal interest which General Sigel took in him he was commissioned a colonel of volunteers. He had had a pretty fair education, a taste for the military profession, and was of tall and slender build, all of which gave him a student-like appearance. He was extremely excitable and nervous when anticipating a crisis, but always calmed down to cool deliberation when the critical moment came. With such a man I could not be less than well satisfied, although the officer whom he replaced—Colonel Laiboldt—had performed efficient service and shown much capacity in the recent campaign.

Colonel G. W. Roberts, of the Forty-Second Illinois Infantry, also came to me in the reorganization. He was an ideal soldier both in mind and body. He was young, tall, handsome, brave, and dashing, and possessed a balance-wheel of such good judgment that in his sphere of action no occasion could arise from which he would not reap the best results. But he too was destined to lay, down his life within a few days, and on the same fatal field. His brigade had been performing garrison duty in Nashville during the siege of that city while Buell's army was in Kentucky, but disliking the prospect of inactivity pending the operations opening before us, Roberts had requested and obtained a transfer to the army in the field. His brigade relieved Colonel Dan McCook's, the latter reluctantly joining the garrison at Nashville, every one in it disappointed and disgusted that the circumstances existing at this time should necessitate their relegation to the harassing and tantalizing duty of protecting our depots and line of supply.

I was fortunate in having such brigade commanders, and no less favored in the regimental and battery commanders. They all were not only patriots, but soldiers, and knowing that discipline must be one of the most potent factors in bringing to a successful termination, the mighty contest in which our nation was struggling for existence, they studied and practiced its methods ceaselessly, inspiring with the same spirit that pervaded themselves the loyal hearts of their subordinate officers and men. All worked unremittingly in the camp at Mill Creek in preparing for the storm, which now plainly indicated its speedy coming. Drills, parades, scouts, foraging expeditions, picket and guard duty, made up the course in this school of instruction, supplemented by frequent changes in the locations of the different brigades, so that the division could have opportunity to learn to break camp quickly and to move out promptly on the march. Foraging expeditions were particularly beneficial in this respect, and when sent out, though absent sometimes for days, the men went without tents or knapsacks, equipped with only one blanket and their arms, ammunition, and rations, to teach them to shift for themselves with slender means in the event of necessity. The number of regimental and headquarters wagons was cut down to the lowest possible figure, and everything made compact by turning into the supply and ammunition trains of the division all surplus transportation, and restricting the personal baggage of officers to the fewest effects possible.

My own staff also was somewhat reorganized and increased at Mill Creek, and though it had been perfectly satisfactory before, yet, on account of the changes of troops that had occurred in the command, I found it necessary to replace valuable officers in some instances, and secure additional ones in others. The gathering of information about the enemy was also industriously pursued, and Card and his brothers were used constantly on expeditions within the Confederate lines, frequently visiting Murfreesboro', Sparta, Tullahoma, Shelbyville, and other points. What they learned was reported to army headquarters, often orally through me or personally communicated by Card himself, but much was forwarded in official letters, beginning with November 24, when I transmitted accurate information of the concentration of Bragg's main force at Tullahoma. Indeed, Card kept me so well posted as to every movement of the enemy, not only with reference to the troops in my immediate front, but also throughout his whole army, that General Rosecrans placed the most unreserved reliance on all his statements, and many times used them to check and correct the reports brought in by his own scouts.

Slight skirmishes took place frequently during this period, and now and then heavy demonstrations were made in the neighborhood of Nolensville by reconnoitring parties from both armies, but none of these ever grew into a battle. These affairs sprung from the desire of each side to feel his antagonist, and had little result beyond emphasizing the fact that behind each line of pickets lay a massed and powerful army busily preparing for the inevitable conflict and eager for its opening. So it wore on till the evening of December 25, 1862; then came the order to move forward.

General Rosecrans, in the reorganization of the army, had assigned Major-General A. McD. McCook to command the right wing, Major-General George H. Thomas the centre, and Major-General T. L. Crittenden the left wing. McCook's wing was made up of three divisions, commanded in order of rank by Brigadier-General Jeff. C. Davis; Brigadier-General R. W. Johnson, and Brigadier-General P. H. Sheridan. Although the corps nomenclature established by General Buell was dropped, the grand divisions into which he had organized the army at Louisville were maintained, and, in fact, the conditions established then remained practically unaltered, with the exception of the interchange of some brigades, the transfer of a few general officers from one wing or division to another, and the substitution of General Thomas for Gilbert as a corps commander. The army was thus compact and cohesive, undisturbed by discord and unembarrassed by jealousies of any moment; and it may be said that under a commander who, we believed, had the energy and skill necessary to direct us to success, a national confidence in our invincibility made us all keen for a test of strength with the Confederates. We had not long to wait.

Early on the morning of December 26, 1862, in a heavy rain, the army marched, the movement being directed on Murfreesboro', where the enemy had made some preparation to go into winter-quarters, and to hold which town it was hoped he would accept battle. General Thomas moved by the Franklin and Wilson pikes, General Crittenden by the Murfreesboro' pike, through Lavergne, and General McCook by the Nolensville pike—Davis's division in advance. As McCook's command neared Nolensville, I received a message from Davis informing me that the Confederates were in considerable force, posted on a range of hills in his front, and requesting me to support him in an attack he was about to make. When the head of my column arrived at Nolensville I began massing my troops on the right of the road, and by the time this formation was nearly completed Davis advanced, but not meeting with sufficient resistance to demand active assistance from me, he with his own command carried the hills, capturing one piece of artillery. This position of the Confederates was a strong one, defending Knob's Gap, through which the Nolensville and Triune pike passed. On the 27th Johnson's division, followed by mine, advanced to Triune, and engaged in a severe skirmish near that place, but my troops were not called into action, the stand made by the enemy being only for the purpose of gaining time to draw in his outlying troops, which done, he retired toward Murfreesboro'. I remained inactive at Triune during the 28th, but early on the 29th moved out by the Bole Jack road to the support of, Davis in his advance to Stewart's Creek, and encamped at Wilkinson's crossroads, from which point to Murfreesboro', distant about six miles, there was a good turnpike. The enemy had sullenly resisted the progress of Crittenden and McCook throughout the preceding three days, and as it was thought probable that he might offer battle at Stewart's Creek, Thomas, in pursuance of his original instructions looking to just such a contingency, had now fallen into the centre by way of the Nolensville crossroads.

On the morning of the 3oth I had the advance of McCook's corps on the Wilkinson pike, Roberts's brigade leading. At first only slight skirmishing took place, but when we came within about three miles of Murfreesboro' the resistance of the enemy's pickets grew serious, and a little further on so strong that I had to put in two regiments to push them back. I succeeded in driving them about half a mile, when I was directed by McCook to form line of battle and place my artillery in position so that I could act in concert with Davis's division, which he wished to post on my right in the general line he desired to take up. In obedience to these directions I deployed on the right of, and oblique to the Wilkinson pike, with a front of four regiments, a second line of four regiments within short supporting distance, and a reserve of one brigade in column of regiments to the rear of my centre. All this time the enemy kept up a heavy artillery and musketry fire on my skirmishers, he occupying, with his sharpshooters, beyond some open fields, a heavy belt of timber to my front and right, where it was intended the left of Davis should finally rest. To gain this point Davis was ordered to swing his division into it in conjunction with a wheeling movement of my right brigade, until our continuous line should face nearly due east. This would give us possession of the timber referred to, and not only rid us of the annoying fire from the skirmishers screened by it, but also place us close in to what was now developing as Bragg's line of battle. The movement was begun about half-past 2, and was successfully executed, after a stubborn resistance. In this preliminary affair the enemy had put in one battery of artillery, which was silenced in a little while, however, by Bush's and Hescock's guns. By sundown I had taken up my prescribed position, facing almost east, my left (Roberts's brigade) resting on the Wilkinson pike, the right (Sill's brigade) in the timber we had just gained, and the reserve brigade (Schaefer's) to the rear of my centre, on some rising ground in the edge of a strip of woods behind Houghtaling's and Hescock's batteries. Davis's division was placed in position on my right, his troops thrown somewhat to the rear, so that his line formed nearly a right angle with mine, while Johnson's division formed in a very exposed position on the right of Davis, prolonging the general line just across the Franklin pike.

The centre, under Thomas, had already formed to my left, the right of Negley's division joining my left in a cedar thicket near the Wilkinson pike, while Crittenden's corps was posted on the left of Thomas, his left resting on Stone River, at a point about two miles and a half from Murfreesboro'.

The precision that had characterized every manoeuvre of the past three days, and the exactness with which each corps and division fell into its allotted place on the evening of the 30th, indicated that at the outset of the campaign a well-digested plan of operations had been prepared for us; and although the scheme of the expected battle was not known to subordinates of my grade, yet all the movements up to this time had been so successfully and accurately made as to give much promise for the morrow, and when night fell there was general anticipation of the best results to the Union army.

CHAPTER XIII.

ASSAULT ON OUR RIGHT FLANK—OCCUPYING A NEW POSITION—THE ENEMY CHECKED—TERRIBLE LOSS OF OFFICERS—AMMUNITION GIVES OUT—RECONSTRUCTING THE LINE—COLLECTING THE WOUNDED AND BURYING THE DEAD—DEALING WITH COWARDS—RESULTS OF THE VICTORY.

The enemy under Bragg lay between us and stone River in order of battle, his general line conforming to the course of that stream. In my immediate front he appeared to be established in strong force in a dense cedar wood, just beyond an open valley, which varied from two hundred to four hundred yards in width, the cedars extending the entire length of the valley. From the events of the day and evening of the 3oth, it was apparent that the two armies were in close proximity, and orders received during the night revealed the fact that Rosecrans intended to attack by throwing his left on the enemy's right, with the expectation of driving it in toward Murfreesboro', so that the right of Crittenden's corps could attack Bragg's centre in reverse, while Thomas supported Crittenden by a simultaneous front assault; and from the movements of the enemy at daylight next morning, it was plainly indicated that Bragg had planned to swing his left on our right by an exactly similar manoeuvre, get possession of the railroad and the Nashville pike, and if possible cut us off from our base at Nashville. The conceptions in the minds of the two generals were almost identical; but Bragg took the initiative, beginning his movement about an hour earlier than the time set by Rosecrans, which gained him an immense advantage in execution in the earlier stages of the action.

During the evening, feeling keenly all the solicitude which attends one in anticipation of a battle, I examined my position with great care, inspecting its whole length several times to remedy any defects that might exist, and to let the men see that I was alive to their interests and advantages. After dark, I went back to the rear of my reserve brigade, and establishing my headquarters behind the trunk of a large fallen tree, which would shelter me somewhat from the cold December wind, lay down beside a small camp-fire to get some rest.

At 2 o'clock on the morning of the 31st General Sill came back to me to report that on his front a continuous movement of infantry and artillery had been going on all night within the Confederate lines, and that he was convinced that Bragg was massing on our right with the purpose of making an attack from that direction early in the morning. After discussing for a few minutes the probabilities of such a course on the part of the enemy, I thought McCook should be made acquainted with what was going on, so Sill and I went back to see him at his headquarters, not far from the Griscom House, where we found him sleeping on some straw in the angle of a worm-fence. I waked him up and communicated the intelligence, and our consequent impressions. He talked the matter over with us for some little time, but in view of the offensive-defensive part he was to play in the coming battle, did not seem to think that there was a necessity for any further dispositions than had already been taken. He said that he thought Johnson's division would be able to take care of the right, and seemed confident that the early assault which was to be made from Rosecrans's left would anticipate and check the designs which we presaged. We two then returned to my little camp-fire behind the log, and as we continued talking of what might be expected from the indications on the right, and Sill becoming more anxious, I directed two regiments from the reserve to report to him, that they might be placed within very short supporting distance of his line. He then rejoined his brigade, better satisfied, but still adhering to the belief he had expressed when first making his report.

Long before dawn my division breakfasted, and was assembled under arms, the infantry in line, the cannoneers at their pieces, but while we were thus preparing, all the recent signs of activity in the enemy's camp were hushed, a death-like stillness prevailing in the cedars to our front. Shortly after daylight General Hardee opened the engagement, just as Sill had predicted, by a fierce attack on Johnson's division, the extreme right of the Union line. Immediate success attending this assault, Hardee extended the attack gradually along in front of Davis, hip movement taking the form of a wheel to the right, the pivot being nearly opposite the left of my division.

Johnson's division soon gave way, and two of Davis's brigades were forced to fall back with it, though stubbornly resisting the determined and sweeping onset.

In the meantime the enemy had also attacked me, advancing across an old cotton-field in Sill's front in heavy masses, which were furiously opened upon by Bush's battery from Sill's line, and by Hescock's and Houghtaling's batteries, which had an oblique fire on the field from a commanding position in rear of my centre. The effect of this fire on the advancing column was terrible, but it continued on till it reached the edge of the timber where Sill's right lay, when my infantry opened at a range of not over fifty yards. For a short time the Confederates withstood the fire, but then wavered, broke, and fell back toward their original line. As they retired, Sill's brigade followed in a spirited charge, driving them back across the open ground and behind their intrenchments. In this charge the gallant Sill was killed; a rifle ball passing through his upper lip and penetrating the brain. Although this was a heavy loss, yet the enemy's discomfiture was such as to give us an hour's time, and as Colonel Greusel, Thirty-sixth Illinois, succeeded to Sill's command, I directed him, as he took charge, to recall the brigade to its original position, for the turning-column on my extreme right was now assuming the most menacing attitude, and it was urgently necessary to prepare for it.

When that portion of the enemy driven back by Sill recovered from its repulse it again advanced to the attack, this time directing its efforts chiefly upon my extreme right, and the front of Woodruff's brigade of Davis's division, which brigade still held on in its first position. In front of my centre the Confederates were again driven back, but as the assault on Woodruff was in conjunction with an advance of the column that had forced Johnson to retire, Woodruff was compelled unfortunately to give way, and two regiments on the right of my line went with him, till they rallied on the two reserve regiments which, in anticipation of the enemy's initiatory attack I had sent to Sill's rear before daylight.

Both Johnson's and Davis's divisions were now practically gone from our line, having retired with a loss of all formation, and they were being closely pursued by the enemy, whose columns were following the arc of a circle that would ultimately carry him in on my rear. In consequence of the fact that this state of things would soon subject me to a fire in reverse, I hastily withdrew Sill's brigade and the reserve regiments supporting it, and ordered Roberts's brigade, which at the close of the enemy's second repulse had changed front toward the south and formed in column of regiments, to cover the withdrawal by a charge on the Confederates as they came into the timber where my right had originally rested. Roberts made the charge at the proper time, and was successful in checking the enemy's advance, thus giving us a breathing-spell, during which I was able to take up a new position with Schaefer's and Sill's brigades on the commanding ground to the rear, where Hescock's and Houghtaling's batteries had been posted all the morning.

The general course of this new position was at right angles with my original line, and it took the shape of an obtuse angle, with my three batteries at the apex. Davis, and Carlin of his division, endeavored to rally their men here on my right, but their efforts were practically unavailing,—though the calm and cool appearance of Carlin, who at the time was smoking a stumpy pipe, had some effect, and was in strong contrast to the excited manner of Davis, who seemed overpowered by the disaster that had befallen his command. But few could be rallied, however, as the men were badly demoralized, and most of them fell back beyond the Wilkinson pike, where they reorganized behind the troops of General Thomas.

At this juncture the enemy's turning-column began advancing again in concert with Cheatham's division, and as the extreme left of the Confederates was directed on Griscom's house, and their right on the Blanton house, my new position was in danger of envelopment. No hope of stemming the tide at this point seemed probable, but to gain time I retained my ground as long as possible, and until, under directions from General McCook, I moved to the front from my left flank and attached myself to the right of Negley's division, which up to this hour had been left almost undisturbed by the enemy in the line it had taken up the night before. Under a heavy fire we succeeded in this manoeuvre, Schaefer's brigade marching first, then the batteries, and Roberts's and Sill's brigades following. When my division arrived on this new ground, I posted Roberts on Negley's right, with Hescock's and Bush's guns, the brigade and guns occupying a low rocky ridge of limestone, which faced them toward Murfreesboro', nearly south. The rest of my division was aligned facing west, along the edge of a cedar thicket, the rear rank backed up on the right flank of Roberts, with Houghtaling's battery in the angle. This presented Sill's and Schaefer's brigades in an almost opposite direction to the line we had so confidently taken up the night before, and covered Negley's rear. The enemy, in the meantime, had continued his wheeling movement till he occupied the ground that my batteries and reserve brigade had held in the morning, and I had now so changed my position that the left brigade of my division approached his intrenchments in front of Stone River, while Sill's and Schaeffer's brigades, by facing nearly west, confronted the successful troops that had smashed in our extreme right.

I had hardly got straightened out in this last place when I was attacked by Cheatham's'division, which, notwithstanding the staggering blows it had previously received from Sill and Roberts, now again moved forward in conjunction with the wheeling movement under the immediate command of Hardee. One of the most sanguinary contests of the day now took place. In fulfillment of Bragg's original design no doubt, Cheatham's division attacked on my left, while heavy masses under Hardee, covered by batteries posted on the high ground formerly occupied by my guns, assaulted my right, the whole force advancing simultaneously. At the same time the enemy opened an artillery fire from his intrenchments in front of Murfreesboro', and it seemed that he was present on every side. My position was strong, however, located in the edge of a dense cedar thicket and commanding a slight depression of open ground that lay in my front. My men were in good spirits too, notwithstanding they had been a good deal hustled around since daylight, with losses that had told considerably on their numbers. Only a short distance now separated the contending lines, and as the batteries on each side were not much more than two hundred yards apart when the enemy made his assault, the artillery fire was fearful in its effect on the ranks of both contestants, the enemy's heavy masses staggering under the torrent of shell and canister from our batteries, while our lines were thinned by his ricochetting projectiles, that rebounded again and again over the thinly covered limestone formation and sped on to the rear of Negley. But all his efforts to dislodge or destroy us were futile, and for the first time since daylight General Hardee was seriously checked in the turning movement he had begun for the purpose of getting possession of the Nashville pike, and though reinforced until two-fifths of Bragg's army was now at his command, yet he met with repulse after repulse, which created great gaps in his lines and taught him that to overwhelm us was hopeless.

As the enemy was recoiling from his first attack, I received a message from Rosecrans telling me that he was making new dispositions, and directing me to hold on where I was until they were completed. From this I judged that the existing conditions of the battle would probably require a sacrifice of my command, so I informed Roberts and Schaefer that we must be prepared to meet the demand on us by withstanding the assault of the enemy, no matter what the outcome. Every energy was therefore bent to the simple holding of our ground, and as ammunition was getting scarce, instructions were given throughout the command to have it reserve its fire till the most effective moment. In a little while came a second and a third assault, and although they were as daring and furious as the first, yet in each case the Confederates were repulsed, driven back in confusion, but not without deadly loss to us, for the noble Roberts was killed, and Colonel Harrington, of the Twenty-Seventh Illinois, who succeeded to his brigade, was mortally wounded a few minutes later. I had now on the death-roll three brigade commanders, and the loss of subordinate officers and men was appalling, but their sacrifice had accomplished the desired result; they had not fallen in vain. Indeed, the bravery and tenacity of my division gave to Rosecrans the time required to make new dispositions, and exacted from our foes the highest commendations.

A lull followed the third fierce assault, and an investigation showed that, with the exception of a few rounds in my brigade, our ammunition was entirely exhausted; and while it was apparent that the enemy was reluctant to renew the conflict in my front, yet I was satisfied I could not hold on much longer without the danger of ultimate capture, so I prepared to withdraw as soon as the troops of Rousseau's division, which had been ordered to take up a line on my right, came into position. Schaefer's and Sill's brigades being without a cartridge, I directed them to fix bayonets for a charge, and await any attempt of the enemy to embarrass my retreat, while Roberts's brigade, offering such resistance as its small quantity of ammunition would permit, was pulled slowly in toward the Nashville pike. Eighty of the horses of Houghtaling's battery having been killed, an attempt was made to bring his guns back by hand over the rocky ground, but it could not be done, and we had to abandon them. Hescock also had lost most of his horses, but all his guns were saved. Bush's battery lost two pieces, the tangled underbrush in the dense cedars proving an obstacle to getting them away which his almost superhuman exertions could not surmount. Thus far the bloody duel had cost me heavily, one-third of my division being killed or wounded. I had already three brigade commanders killed; a little later I lost my fourth—Colonel Schaefer.

The difficulties of withdrawing were very great, as the ground was exceptionally rocky, and the growth of cedars almost impenetrable for wheeled carriages. Retiring sullenly under a heavy fire, while the general line was reformed to my right and rear, my division was at length drawn through the cedars and debouched into an open space near the Murfreesboro' pike, behind the right of Palmer's division. Two regiments of Sill's brigade, however, on account of the conformation of the ground, were obliged to fall back from the point where Woodruff's brigade of Davis's division had rallied after the disaster of the early morning. The division came out of the cedars with unbroken ranks, thinned by only its killed and wounded—but few missing. When we came into the open ground, McCook directed Roberts's brigade—now commanded by Colonel Luther P. Bradley—to proceed a short distance to the rear on the Nashville pike, to repel the enemy's threatening attempt at our communications. Willingly and cheerfully the brigade again entered the fight under these new conditions, and although it was supplied with but three or four cartridges to the man now, it charged gallantly and recaptured two pieces of artillery which the Union troops had had to abandon at that point.

Shortly after we debouched from the cedars I was directed by Rosecrans to send some aid to the right of General Palmer's division; and two of Schaefer's regiments, having obtained ammunition, were pushed up on Palmer's right, accompanied by four of Hescock's guns; but the advance of the enemy here had already been checked by Palmer, and only a desultory contest ensued. Rosecrans, whom I now met in the open ground west of the railroad, behind Palmer, directed that my command should relieve Wood's division, which was required to fall back and take up the new line that had been marked out while I was holding on in the cedars. His usually florid face had lost its ruddy color, and his anxious eyes told that the disasters of the morning were testing his powers to the very verge of endurance, but he seemed fully to comprehend what had befallen us. His firmly set lips and, the calmness with which his instructions were delivered inspired confidence in all around him; and expressing approbation of what my division had done, while deliberately directing it to a new point, he renewed in us all the hope of final victory, though it must be admitted that at this phase of the battle the chances lay largely with the enemy.

Withdrawing the two regiments and Hescock's battery, that I had posted on the right of Palmer, I moved as directed by Rosecrans into the position to the east of the railroad, and formed immediately to the right of Wood, who was now being attacked all along his front, but more particularly where his right rested near the railroad. Under a storm of shot and shell that came in torrents my troops took up the new ground, advancing through a clump of open timber to Wood's assistance. Forming in line in front of the timber we poured a telling fire into the enemy's ranks, which were then attacking across some cleared fields; but when he discovered additional troops confronting him, he gave up the attempt to carry Wood's position. It was here that I lost Schaefer, who was killed instantly, making my fourth brigade commander dead that day. The enemy in front of Wood having been checked, our whole line east of the railroad executed undisturbed its retrograde movement to a position about three hundred yards to its rear. When I fell back to the edge of the clump of timber, where when first coming on the ground I had formed to help Wood, I was ordered by Rosecrans to prepare to make a charge should the enemy again assault us. In anticipation of this work I massed my troops in close column. The expected attack never came, however, but the shot and shell of a furious cannonade told with fatal effect upon men and officers as they lay on their faces hugging the ground. The torments of this trying situation were almost unbearable, but it was obvious to all that it was necessary to have at hand a compact body of troops to repel any assault the enemy might make pending the reconstruction of the extreme right of our line, and a silent determination to stay seemed to take hold of each individual soldier; nor was this grim silence interrupted throughout the cannonade, except in one instance, when one of the regiments broke out in a lusty cheer as a startled rabbit in search of a new hiding-place safely ran the whole length of the line on the backs of the men.

While my troops were still lying here, General Rosecrans, with a part of his staff and a few orderlies, rode out on the rearranged line to supervise its formation and encourage the men, and in prosecution of these objects moved around the front of my column of attack, within range of the batteries that were shelling us so viciously. As he passed to the open ground on my left, I joined him. The enemy seeing this mounted party, turned his guns upon it, and his accurate aim was soon rewarded, for a solid shot carried away the head of Colonel Garesche, the chief-of-staff, and killed or wounded two or three orderlies. Garesche's appalling death stunned us all, and a momentary expression of horror spread over Rosecrans's face; but at such a time the importance of self-control was vital, and he pursued his course with an appearance of indifference, which, however, those immediately about him saw was assumed, for undoubtedly he felt most deeply the death of his friend and trusted staff-officer.

No other attacks were made on us to the east of the railroad for the rest of the afternoon, and just before dark I was directed to withdraw and take up a position along the west side of the Nashville pike, on the extreme right of our new line, where Roberts's brigade and the Seventy-third and Eighty-eighth Illinois had already been placed by McCook. The day had cost me much anxiety and sadness, and I was sorely disappointed at the general result, though I could not be other than pleased at the part taken by my command. The loss of my brigade commanders—Sill, Roberts, Schaefer, and Harrington-and a large number of regimental and battery officers, with so many of their men, struck deep into my heart: My thinned ranks told the woeful tale of the fierce struggles, indescribable by words, through which my division had passed since 7 o'clock in the morning; and this, added to our hungry and exhausted condition, was naturally disheartening. The men had been made veterans, however, by the fortunes and misfortunes of the day, and as they went into their new places still confident of final success, it was plain to see that they felt a self-confidence inspired by the part they had already played.

My headquarters were now established on the Nashville pike, about three miles and a half from Murfreesboro'; my division being aligned to the west of the pike, bowed out and facing almost west, Cleburn's division of the Confederates confronting it. Davis's division was posted on my right, and Walker's brigade of Thomas's corps, which had reported to me, took up a line that connected my left with Johnson's division.

Late in the evening General Rosecrans, accompanied by General McCook, and several other officers whose names I am now unable to recall, rode by my headquarters on their way to the rear to look for a new line of battle—on Overall's creek it was said—that would preserve our communications with Nashville and offer better facilities for resistance than the one we were now holding. Considerable time had elapsed when they returned from this exploration and proceeded to their respective commands, without intimating to me that anything had been determined upon by the reconnoissance, but a little later it was rumored through the different headquarters that while the party was looking for a new position it discovered the enemy's troops moving toward our right and rear, the head of his columns being conducted in the darkness by the aid of torches, and that no alternative was left us but to hold the lines we then occupied. The torches had been seen unquestionably, and possibly created some alarm at first in the minds of the reconnoitring party, but it was soon ascertained that the lights came from a battalion of the Fourth regular cavalry that was picketing our flank and happened to be starting its bivouac fires at the moment. The fires and the supposed movements had no weight, therefore, in deciding the proposition to take up a line at Overall's creek, but General Rosecrans, fortunately for the army, decided to remain where he was. Doubtless reflections during his ride caused him to realize that the enemy must be quite as much crippled as himself. If it had been decided to fall back to Overall's creek, we could have withdrawn without much difficulty very likely, but such a retrograde movement would have left to the enemy the entire battle-field of Stone River and ultimately compelled our retreat to Nashville.

In the night of December 3rd several slight demonstrations were made on my front, but from the darkness neither party felt the effect of the other's fire, and when daylight came again the skirmishers and lines of battle were in about the same position they had taken up the evening before. Soon after daybreak it became evident that the conflict was to be renewed, and a little later the enemy resumed the offensive by an attack along my left front, especially on Walker's brigade. His attempt was ineffectual, however, and so easily repulsed as to demonstrate that the desperate character of his assaults the day before had nearly exhausted his strength. About 3 o'clock in the afternoon he made another feeble charge on my front, but our fire from the barricades and rifle-pits soon demoralized his advancing lines, which fell back in some confusion, thus enabling us to pick up about a hundred prisoners. From this time till the evening of January 3 Bragg's left remained in our front, and continued to show itself at intervals by weak demonstrations, which we afterward ascertained were directly intended to cover the desperate assault he made with Breckenridge on the left of Rosecrans, an assault that really had in view only a defensive purpose, for unless Bragg dislodged the troops which were now massing in front of his right he would be obliged to withdraw General Polk's corps behind Stone River and finally abandon Murfreesboro'. The sequel proved this to be the case; and the ill-judged assault led by Breckenridge ending in entire defeat, Bragg retired from Murfreesboro' the night of January 3.

General Rosecrans occupied Murfreesboro' on the 4th and 5th, having gained a costly victory, which was not decisive enough in its character to greatly affect the general course of the war, though it somewhat strengthened and increased our hold on Middle Tennessee. The enemy in retiring did not fall back very far—only behind Duck River to Shelbyville and Tullahoma—and but little endeavor was made to follow him. Indeed, we were not in condition to pursue, even if it had been the intention at the outset of the campaign.

As soon as possible after the Confederate retreat I went over the battle-field to collect such of my wounded as had not been carried off to the South and to bury my dead. In the cedars and on the ground where I had been so fiercely assaulted when the battle opened, on the morning of the 31st, evidences of the bloody struggle appeared on every hand in the form of broken fire-arms, fragments of accoutrements, and splintered trees. The dead had nearly all been left unburied, but as there was likelihood of their mutilation by roving swine, the bodies had mostly been collected in piles at different points and inclosed by rail fences. The sad duties of interment and of caring for the wounded were completed by the 5th, and on the 6th I moved my division three miles, south of Murfreesboro' on the Shelbyville pike, going into camp on the banks of Stone River. Here the condition of my command was thoroughly looked into, and an endeavor made to correct such defects as had been disclosed by the recent battle.

During the engagement there had been little straggling, and my list of missing was small and legitimate; still, it was known that a very few had shirked their duty, and an example was necessary. Among this small number were four officers who, it was charged, had abandoned their colors and regiments. When their guilt was clearly established, and as soon as an opportunity occurred, I caused the whole division to be formed in a hollow square, closed in mass, and had the four officers marched to the centre, where, telling them that I would not humiliate any officer or soldier by requiring him to touch their disgraced swords, I compelled them to deliver theirs up to my colored servant, who also cut from their coats every insignia of rank. Then, after there had been read to the command an order from army headquarters dismissing the four from the service, the scene was brought to a close by drumming the cowards out of camp. It was a mortifying spectacle, but from that day no officer in that division ever abandoned his colors.

My effective force in the battle of Stone River was 4,154 officers and men. Of this number I lost 1,633 killed, wounded, and missing, or nearly 40 per cent. In the remaining years of the war, though often engaged in most severe contests, I never experienced in any of my commands so high a rate of casualties. The ratio of loss in the whole of Rosecrans's army was also high, and Bragg's losses were almost equally great. Rosecrans carried into the action about 42,000 officers and men. He lost 13,230, or 31 per cent. Bragg's effective force was 37,800 officers and men; he lost 10,306, or nearly 28 per cent.

Though our victory was dearly bought, yet the importance of gaining the day at any price was very great, particularly when we consider what might have been the result had not the gallantry of the army and the manoeuvring during the early disaster saved us from ultimate defeat. We had started out from Nashville on an offensive campaign, probably with no intention of going beyond Murfreesboro', in midwinter, but still with the expectation of delivering a crushing blow should the enemy accept our challenge to battle. He met us with a plan of attack almost the counterpart of our own. In the execution of his plan he had many advantages, not the least of which was his intimate knowledge of the ground, and he came near destroying us. Had he done so, Nashville would probably have fallen; at all events, Kentucky would have been opened again to his incursions, and the theatre of war very likely transferred once more to the Ohio River. As the case now stood, however, Nashville was firmly established as a base for future operations, Kentucky was safe from the possibility of being again overrun, and Bragg, thrown on the defensive, was compelled to give his thoughts to the protection of the interior of the Confederacy and the security of Chattanooga, rather than indulge in schemes of conquest north of the Cumberland River. While he still held on in Middle Tennessee his grasp was so much loosened that only slight effort would be necessary to push him back into Georgia, and thus give to the mountain region of East Tennessee an opportunity to prove its loyalty to the, Union.

The victory quieted the fears of the West and Northwest, destroyed the hopes of the secession element in Kentucky, renewed the drooping spirits of the East Tennesseans, and demoralized the disunionists in Middle Tennessee; yet it was a negative victory so far as concerned the result on the battle-field. Rosecrans seems to have planned the battle with the idea that the enemy would continue passive, remain entirely on the defensive, and that it was necessary only to push forward our left in order to force the evacuation of Murfreesboro'; and notwithstanding the fact that on the afternoon of December 30 McCook received information that the right of Johnson's division. resting near the Franklin pike, extended only to about the centre of the Confederate army, it does not appear that attack from that quarter was at all apprehended by the Union commanders.

The natural line of retreat of the Confederates was not threatened by the design of Rosecrans; and Bragg, without risk to his communications, anticipated it by a counter-attack of like character from his own left, and demolished his adversary's plan the moment we were thrown on the defensive. Had Bragg followed up with the spirit which characterized its beginning the successful attack by Hardee on our right wing—and there seems no reason why he should not have done so—the army of Rosecrans still might have got back to Nashville, but it would have been depleted and demoralized to such a degree as to unfit it for offensive operations for a long time afterward. Bragg's intrenchments in front of Stone River were very strong, and there seems no reason why he should not have used his plain advantage as explained, but instead he allowed us to gain time, intrench, and recover a confidence that at first was badly shaken. Finally, to cap the climax of his errors, he directed Breckenridge to make the assault from his right flank on January 2, with small chance for anything but disaster, when the real purpose in view could have been accomplished without the necessity of any offensive manoeuvre whatever.

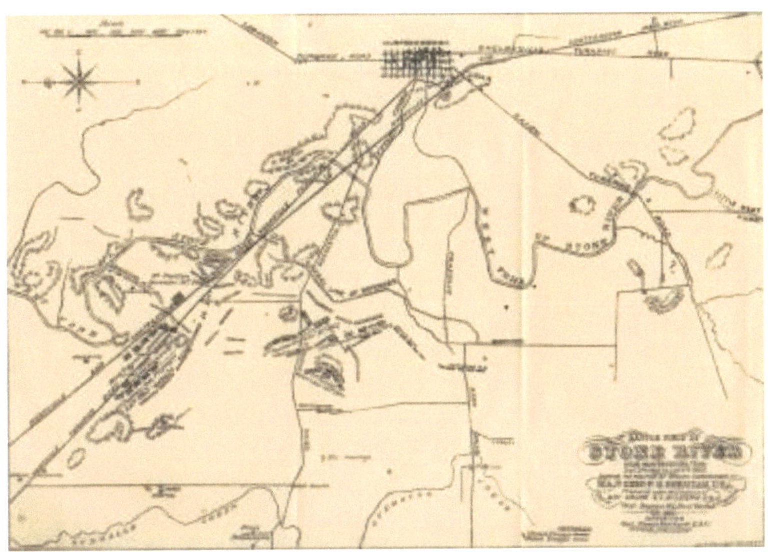

Enlarge

CHAPTER XIV.

On the 6th of January, 1863, my division settled quietly down in its camp south of Murfreesboro'. Its exhausted condition after the terrible experiences of the preceding week required attention. It needed recuperation, reinforcement, and reorganization, and I set about these matters without delay, in anticipation of active operations early in the spring. No forward movement was made for nearly six months, however, and throughout this period drills, parades, reconnoissances, and foraging expeditions filled in the time profitably. In addition to these exercises the construction of permanent fortifications for the security of Murfreesboro' was undertaken by General Rosecrans, and large details from my troops were furnished daily for the work. Much attention was also given to creating a more perfect system of guard and picket duty-a matter that had hitherto been somewhat neglected in the army, as its constant activity had permitted scant opportunity for the development of such a system. It was at this time that I received my appointment as a major-general of Volunteers. My promotion had been recommended by General Rosecrans immediately after the battle of Stone River, but for some reason it was delayed until April, and though a long time elapsed between the promise and the performance, my gratification was extreme.

My scout, Card, was exceedingly useful while encamped near Murfreesboro, making several trips to East Tennessee within the enemy's lines to collect information as to the condition of the loyal people there, and to encourage them with the hope of early liberation. He also brought back from each trip very accurate statements as to the strength and doings of the Confederate army, fixing almost with certainty its numbers and the locations of its different divisions, and enabling my engineer-officer—Major Morhardt—to construct good maps of the country in our front. On these dangerous excursions Card was always accompanied by one of his brothers, the other remaining with me to be ready for duty if any accident occurred to those who had gone out, or in case I wanted to communicate with them. In this way we kept well posted, although the intelligence these men brought was almost always secured at the risk of their lives.

Early in the spring, before the Tullahoma campaign began, I thought it would be practicable, by sending out a small secret expedition of but three or four men, to break the Nashville and Chattanooga railroad between Chattanooga and the enemy's position at Tullahoma by burning the bridges in Crow Creek valley from its head to Stevenson, Alabama, and then the great bridge across the Tennessee River at Bridgeport. Feeling confident that I could persuade Card to undertake the perilous duty, I broached the contemplated project to him, and he at once jumped at the opportunity of thus distinguishing himself, saying that with one of his brothers and three other loyal East Tennesseeans, whose services he knew could be enlisted, he felt sure of carrying out the idea, so I gave him authority to choose his own assistants. In a few days his men appeared at my headquarters, and when supplied with money in notes of the State Bank of Tennessee, current everywhere as gold in those days, the party, composed of Card, the second brother, and the three East Tennesseeans, started on their precarious enterprise, their course being directed first toward the Cumberland Mountains, intending to strike the Nashville and Chattanooga railroad somewhere above Anderson's station. They expected to get back in about fifteen days, but I looked for some knowledge of the progress of their adventure before the expiration of that period, hoping to hear through Confederate sources prisoners and the like-of the destruction of the bridges. I waited in patience for such news, but none came, and as the time Card had allotted himself passed by, I watched anxiously for his return, for, as there was scarcely a doubt that the expedition had proved a failure, the fate of the party became a matter of deep concern to Card's remaining brother and to me. Finally this brother volunteered to go to his father's house in East Tennessee to get tidings of the party, and I consented, for the probabilities were that some of them had made their way to that point, or at least that some information had reached there about them. As day after day went by, the time fixed for this brother's return came round, yet he also remained out; but some days after the lad was due Card himself turned up accompanied by the brother he had taken with him, soon explained his delay in getting back, and gave me the story of his adventures while absent.

After leaving my camp, his party had followed various byways across the Cumberland Mountains to Crow Creek Valley, as instructed; but when nearing the railroad above Anderson's Station, they were captured by some guerrillas prowling about that vicinity, and being suspected of disloyalty to the Confederacy, were carried to Chattanooga and imprisoned as Yankee spies. Their prospects now were decidedly discouraging, for death stared them in the face. Fortunately, however, some delays occurred relative to the disposition that should be made of them, and they, meanwhile, effected their escape from their jailors by way of one of the prison windows, from which they managed to displace a bar, and by a skiff, in the darkness of night, crossed the Tennessee River a little below Chattanooga. From this point the party made their way back to my camp, traveling only at night, hiding in the woods by day, and for food depending on loyal citizens that Card had become acquainted with when preaching and peddling.

Card's first inquiry after relating his story was for the youngest brother, whom he had left with me. I told him what I had done, in my anxiety about himself, and that more than sufficient time had elapsed for his brother's return. His reply was: "They have caught him. The poor fellow is dead." His surmise proved correct; for news soon came that the poor boy had been captured at his father's house, and hanged. The blow to Card was a severe one, and so hardened his heart against the guerrillas in the neighborhood of his father's home—for he knew they were guilty of his brother's murder—that it was with difficulty I could persuade him to continue in the employment of the Government, so determined was he to avenge his brother's death at the first opportunity. Finally, however, I succeeded in quieting the almost uncontrollable rage that seemed to possess him, and he remained with me during the Tullahoma and Chickamauga campaigns; but when we reached Knoxville the next winter, he took his departure, informing me that he was going

for the bushwhackers who had killed his brother. A short time after
he left me, I saw him at the head of about thirty well-armed East
Tennesseeans — refugees. They were determined-looking men, seeking revenge for the wrongs and sufferings that had been put upon
them in the last two years, and no doubt wreaked their vengeance
right and left on all who had been in any way instrumental in per-
secuting them.

The feeding of our army from the base at Louisville was attended
with a great many difficulties, as the enemy's cavalry was constantly breaking the railroad and intercepting our communications on
the Cumberland River at different points that were easily accessible
to his then superior force of troopers. The accumulation of reserve
stores was therefore not an easy task, and to get forage ahead a few
days was well-nigh impossible, unless that brought from the North
was supplemented by what we could gather from the country. Corn
was abundant in the region to the south and southwest of
Murfreesboro', so to make good our deficiences in this respect, I
employed a brigade about once a week in the duty of collecting and
bringing in forage, sending out sometimes as many as a hundred
and fifty wagons to haul the grain which my scouts had previously
located. In nearly every one of these expeditions the enemy was
encountered, and the wagons were usually loaded while the skirmishers kept up a running fire, Often there would occur a respecta-
ble brush, with the loss on each side of a number of killed and
wounded. The officer in direct command always reported to me
personally whatever had happened during the time he was out —
the result of his reconnoissance, so to speak, for that war the real
nature of these excursions — and on one occasion the colonel in
command, Colonel Conrad, of the Fifteenth Missouri, informed me
that he got through without much difficulty; in fact, that everything
had gone all right and been eminently satisfactory, except that in
returning he had been mortified greatly by the conduct of the two
females belonging to the detachment and division train at my headquarters. These women, he said, had given much annoyance by
getting drunk, and to some extent demoralizing his men. To say
that I was astonished at his statement would be a mild way of putting it, and had I not known him to be a most upright man and of
sound sense, I should have doubted not only his veracity, but his

sanity. Inquiring who they were and for further details, I was informed that there certainly were in the command two females, that in some mysterious manner had attached themselves to the service as soldiers; that one, an East Tennessee woman, was a teamster in the division wagon-train and the other a private soldier in a cavalry company temporarily attached to my headquarters for escort duty. While out on the foraging expedition these Amazons had secured a supply of "apple-jack" by some means, got very drunk, and on the return had fallen into Stone River and been nearly drowned. After they had been fished from, the water, in the process of resuscitation their sex was disclosed, though up to this time it appeared to be known only to each other. The story was straight and the circumstance clear, so, convinced of Conrad's continued sanity, I directed the provost-marshal to bring in arrest to my headquarters the two disturbers of Conrad's peace of mind, After some little search the East Tennessee woman was found in camp, somewhat the worse for the experiences of the day before, but awaiting her fate content idly smoking a cob-pipe. She was brought to me, and put in duress under charge of the division surgeon until her companion could be secured. To the doctor she related that the year before she had "refugeed" from East Tennessee, and on arriving in Louisville assumed men's apparel and sought and obtained employment as a teamster in the quartermaster's department. Her features were very large, and so coarse and masculine was her general appearance that she would readily have passed as a man, and in her case the deception was no doubt easily practiced. Next day the "she dragoon" was caught, and proved to be a rather prepossessing young woman, and though necessarily bronzed and hardened by exposure, I doubt if, even with these marks of campaigning, she could have deceived as readily as did her companion. How the two got acquainted, I never learned, and though they had joined the army independently of each other, yet an intimacy had sprung up between them long before the mishaps of the foraging expedition. They both were forwarded to army headquarters, and, when provided with clothing suited to their sex, sent back to Nashville, and thence beyond our lines to Louisville.

On January 9, by an order from the War Department, the Army of the Cumberland had been divided into three corps, designated the

Fourteenth, Twentieth, and Twenty-first. This order did not alter the composition of the former grand divisions, nor change the commanders, but the new nomenclature was a decided improvement over the clumsy designations Right Wing, Centre, and Left Wing, which were well calculated to lead to confusion sometimes. McCook's wing became the Twentieth Corps, and my division continued of the same organization, and held the same number as formerly-the Third Division, Twentieth Corps. My first brigade was now commanded by Brigadier-General William H. Lytle, the second by Colonel Bernard Laiboldt, and the third by Colonel Luther P. Bradley.

On the 4th of March I was directed to move in light marching order toward Franklin and join General Gordon Granger, to take part in some operations which he was projecting against General Earl Van Dorn, then at Spring Hill. Knowing that my line of march would carry me through a region where forage was plentiful, I took along a large train of empty wagons, which I determined to fill with corn and send back to Murfreesboro', believing that I could successfully cover the train by Minty's brigade of cavalry, which had joined me for the purpose of aiding in a reconnoissance toward Shelbyville. In marching the column I placed a regiment of infantry at its head, then the wagon-train, then a brigade of infantry — masking the cavalry behind this brigade. The enemy, discovering that the train was with us, and thinking he could capture it, came boldly out with his, cavalry to attack. The head of his column came up to the crossroads at Versailles, but holding him there, I passed the train and infantry brigade beyond toward Eagleville, and when my cavalry had been thus unmasked, Minty, followed by the balance of my division, which was still behind, charged him with the sabre. Success was immediate and complete, and pursuit of the routed forces continued through Unionville, until we fell upon and drove in the Confederate outposts at Shelbyville. Here the enemy was taken by surprise evidently, which was most fortunate for us, otherwise the consequences might have been disastrous. Minty captured in the charge about fifty prisoners and a few wagons and mules, and thus enabled me to load my train with corn, and send it back to Murfreesboro' unmolested. In this little fight the sabre was freely used by both sides, and I do not believe that during the whole war I again knew of so large a percentage of wounds by that arm in proportion to the numbers engaged.

That night I encamped at Eagleville, and next day reported to Granger at Franklin, arriving in the midst of much excitement prevailing on account of the loss of Coburn's brigade, which had been captured the day before a little distance south of that point, while marching to form a junction with a column that had been directed on Columbia from Murfreesboro'. Shortly after Coburn's capture General Granger had come upon the scene, and the next day he advanced my division and Minty's troops directly on Spring Hill, with a view to making some reprisal; but Van Dorn had no intention of accommodating us, and retired from Spring Hill, offering but little resistance. He continued to fall back, till finally he got behind Duck River, where operations against him ceased; for, in consequence of the incessant rains of the season, the streams had become almost impassable. Later, I returned by way of Franklin to my old camp at Murfreesboro', passing over on this march the ground on which the Confederate General Hood met with such disaster the following year in his attack on Stanley's corps.

My command had all returned from the Franklin expedition to Murfreesboro' and gone into camp on the Salem pike by the latter part of March, from which time till June it took part in only the little affairs of outposts occurring every now and then on my own front. In the meanwhile General Rosecrans had been materially reinforced by the return of sick and wounded men; his army had become well disciplined, and was tolerably supplied; and he was repeatedly pressed by the authorities at Washington to undertake offensive operations.

During the spring and early summer Rosecrans resisted, with a great deal of spirit and on various grounds, these frequent urgings, and out of this grew up an acrimonious correspondence and strained feeling between him and General Halleck. Early in June, however, stores had been accumulated and other preparations made for a move forward, Resecrans seeming to have decided that he could safely risk an advance, with the prospect of good results. Before finally deciding, he called upon most of his corps and division commanders for their opinions on certain propositions which he presented, and most of them still opposed the projected movement, I among the number, reasoning that while General Grant was operating against Vicksburg, it was better to hold Bragg in Middle Tennessee than to push him so far back into Georgia that interior means of communication would give the Confederate Government the opportunity of quickly joining a part of his force to that of General Johnson in Mississippi.

At this stage, and in fact prior to it, Rosecrans seemed to manifest special confidence in me, often discussing his plans with me independent of the occasions on which he formally referred them for my views. I recollect that on two different occasions about this time he unfolded his designs to me in this informal way, outlining generally how he expected ultimately to force Bragg south of the Tennessee River, and going into the details of the contemplated move on Tullahoma. His schemes, to my mind, were not only comprehensive, but exact, and showed conclusively, what no one doubted then, that they were original with him. I found in them very little to criticise unfavorably, if we were to move at all, and Rosecrans certainly impressed me that he favored an advance at an early day, though many of his generals were against it until the operations on the Mississippi River should culminate in something definite. There was much, fully apparent in the circumstances about his headquarters, leading to the conviction that Rosecrans originated the Tullahoma campaign, and the record of his prior performances collaterally sustains the visible evidence then existing. In my opinion, then, based on a clear recollection of various occurrences growing out of our intimacy, he conceived the plan of the Tullahoma campaign and the one succeeding it; and is therefore entitled to every credit that attended their execution, no matter what may be claimed for others.

On the 23d of June Bragg was covering his position north of Duck River with a front extending from McMinnville, where his cavalry rested, through Wartrace and Shelbyville to Columbia, his depot being at Tullahoma. Rosecrans, thinking that Bragg would offer strong resistance at Shelbyville — which was somewhat protected by a spur of low mountains or hills, offshoots of the Cumberland Mountains — decided to turn that place; consequently, he directed the mass of the Union army on the enemy's right flank, about Manchester.

On the 26th of June McCook's corps advanced toward Liberty Gap, my divisions marching on the Shelbyville pike. I had proceeded but a few miles when I encountered the enemy's pickets, who fell back to Christiana, about nine miles from Murfreesboro'. Here I was assailed pretty wickedly by the enemy's sharpshooters and a section of artillery, but as I was instructed to do nothing more than cover the road from Eagleville, over which Brannan's division was to approach Christiana, I made little reply to this severe annoyance, wishing to conceal the strength of my force. As soon as the head of Brannan's column arrived I marched across-country to the left, and encamped that night at the little town of Millersburg, in the vicinity of Liberty Gap. I was directed to move from Millersburg, on Hoover's Gap—a pass in the range of hills already referred to, through which ran the turnpike from Murfreesboro' to Manchester—but heavy rains had made the country roads almost impassable, and the last of my division did not reach Hoover's Gap till the morning of June 27, after its abandonment by the enemy. Continuing on to Fairfield, the head of my column met, south of that place, a small force of Confederate infantry and cavalry, which after a slight skirmish Laiboldt's brigade drove back toward Wartrace. The next morning I arrived at Manchester, where I remained quiet for the day. Early on the 29th I marched by the Lynchburg road for Tullahoma, where the enemy was believed to be in force, and came into position about six miles from the town.

By the 31st the whole army had been concentrated, in spite of many difficulties, and though, on account of the heavy rains that had fallen almost incessantly since we left Murfreesboro', its movements had been slow and somewhat inaccurate, yet the precision with which it took up a line of battle for an attack on Tullahoma showed that forethought and study had been given to every detail. The enemy had determined to fall back from Tullahoma at the beginning of the campaign, however, and as we advanced, his evacuation had so far progressed that when, on July 1. We reached the earthworks thrown. up early in the year for the defense of the place, he had almost wholly disappeared, carrying off all his stores and munitions of war except some little subsistence and eleven pieces of artillery. A strong rearguard remained to cover the retreat, and on my front the usual encounters between advancing and retreating forces took place. Just before reaching the intrenchments on the Lynchburg road, I came upon an open space that was covered by a network of fallen trees and underbrush, which had been slashed all along in front of the enemy's earthworks. This made our progress very difficult, but I shortly became satisfied that there were only a few of the enemy within the works, so moving a battalion of cavalry that had joined me the day before down the road as rapidly as the obstructions would permit, the Confederate pickets quickly departed, and we gained possession of the town. Three siege guns, four caissons, a few stores, and a small number of prisoners fell into my hands.

That same evening orders were issued to the army to push on from Tullahoma in pursuit, for, as it was thought that we might not be able to cross Elk River on account of its swollen condition, we could do the enemy some damage by keeping close as possible at his heels. I marched on the Winchester road at 3 o'clock on the 2d of July and about 8 o'clock reached Elk River ford. The stream was for the time truly an impassable torrent, and all hope of crossing by the Winchester ford had to be abandoned. Deeming that further effort should be made, however, under guidance of Card, I turned the head of my column in the direction of Alisona, marching up the river and nearly parallel with it till I came to Rock Creek. With a little delay we got across Rock Creek, which was also much swollen, and finding a short distance above its mouth a ford on Elk River that Card said was practicable, I determined to attempt it: Some of the enemy's cavalry were guarding this ford, but after a sharp little skirmish my battalion of cavalry crossed and took up a strong position on the other bank. The stream was very high and the current very swift, the water, tumbling along over its rocky bed in an immense volume, but still it was fordable for infantry if means could be devised by which the men could keep their feet. A cable was stretched across just below the ford as a lifeline for the weaker ones, and then the men of the entire division having secured their ammunition by placing the cartridge-boxes on their shoulders, the column pushed cheerfully into the rushing current. The men as they entered the water joined each other in sets of four in a close embrace, which enabled them to retain a foothold and successfully resist the force of the flood. When they were across I turned the column down the left bank of Elk River, and driving the enemy from some slight works near Estelle Springs, regained the Winchester road.

By this time it was clear that Bragg intended to fall back behind the Tennessee River, and our only chance of accomplishing anything of importance was to smash up his rear-guard before it crossed the Cumberland Mountains, and in pursuance of this idea I was directed to attack such of his force as was holding on to Winchester. At 4 o'clock on the morning of July 2 I moved on that town, and when we got close to it directed my mounted troops to charge a small force of Confederate cavalry that was picketing their front. The Confederates resisted but little, and our men went with them in a disorderly chase through the village to Boiling Fork, a small stream about half a mile beyond. Here the fleeing pickets, rallying behind a stronger force, made a stand, and I was directed by McCook to delay till I ascertained if Davis's division, which was to support me, had made the crossing of Elk River, and until I could open up communication with Brannan's division, which was to come in on my left at Decherd. As soon as I learned that Davis was across I pushed on, but the delay had permitted the enemy to pull his rear-guard up on the mountain, and rendered nugatory all further efforts to hurt him materially, our only returns consisting in forcing him to relinquish a small amount of transportation and forage at the mouth of the pass just beyond Cowan, a station on the line of the Nashville and Chattanooga railroad.

At Cowan, Colonel Watkins, of the Sixth Kentucky Cavalry, reported to me with twelve hundred mounted men. Having heard during the night that the enemy had halted on the mountain near the University—an educational establishment on the summit—I directed Watkins to make a reconnoissance and find out the value of the information. He learned that Wharton's brigade of cavalry was halted at the University to cover a moderately large force of the enemy's infantry which had not yet got down the mountain on the other side, so I pushed Watkins out again on the 5th, supporting him by a brigade of infantry, which I accompanied myself. We were too late, however, for when we arrived at the top of the mountain Wharton had disappeared, and though Watkins pursued to Bridgeport, he was able to do nothing more, and on his return reported that the last of the enemy had crossed the Tennessee River and burned the railroad bridge.

Nothing further could now be done, so I instructed Watkins to rejoin the division at Cowan, and being greatly fatigued by the hard campaigning of the previous ten days, I concluded to go back to my camp in a more comfortable way than on the back of my tired horse. In his retreat the enemy had not disturbed the railway track at all, and as we had captured a hand-car at Cowan, I thought I would have it brought up to the station near the University to carry me down the mountain to my camp, and, desiring company, I persuasively invited Colonel Frank T. Sherman to ride with me. I sent for the car by a courier, and for a long time patiently awaited its arrival, in fact, until all the returning troops had passed us, but still it did not come. Thinking it somewhat risky to remain at the station without protection, Sherman and myself started our horses to Cowan by our orderlies, and set out on foot to meet the car, trudging along down the track in momentary expectation of falling in with our private conveyance. We had not gone very far before night overtook us, and we then began to realize the dangers surrounding us, for there we were alone and helpless, tramping on in the darkness over an unknown railroad track in the enemy's country, liable on the one hand to go tumbling through some bridge or trestle, and on the other, to possible capture or death at the hands of the guerrillas then infesting these mountains. Just after dark we came to a little cabin near the track, where we made bold to ask for water, notwithstanding the fact that to disclose ourselves to the inmates might lead to fatal consequences. The water was kindly given, but the owner and his family were very much exercised lest some misfortune might befall us near their house, and be charged to them, so they encouraged us to move on with a frankness inspired by fear of future trouble to themselves.

At every turn we eagerly hoped to meet the hand-car, but it never came, and we jolted on from tie to tie for eleven weary miles, reaching Cowan after midnight, exhausted and sore in every muscle from frequent falls on the rough, unballasted road-bed. Inquiry. developed that the car had been well manned, and started to us as ordered, and nobody could account for its non-arrival. Further investigation next day showed, however, that when it reached the foot of the mountain, where the railroad formed a junction, the improvised crew, in the belief no doubt that the University was on the main line instead of near the branch to Tracy City, followed the main stem until it carried them clear across the range down the Crow Creek Valley, where the party was captured.

I had reason to remember for many a day this foolish adventure, for my sore bones and bruised muscles, caused me physical suffering until I left the Army of the Cumberland the next spring; but I had still more reason to feel for my captured men, and on this account I have never ceased to regret that I so thoughtlessly undertook to rejoin my troops by rail, instead of sticking to my faithful horse.

CHAPTER XV.

The Tullahoma campaign was practically closed by the disappearance of the enemy from the country north of the Tennessee River. Middle Tennessee was once more in the possession of the National troops, and Rosecrans though strongly urged from Washington to continue on, resisted the pressure until he could repair the Nashville and Chattanooga railroad, which was of vital importance in supplying his army from its secondary base at Nashville. As he desired to hold this road to where it crossed the Tennessee, it was necessary to push a force beyond the mountains, and after a few days of rest at Cowan my division was ordered to take station at Stevenson, Alabama, the junction of the Memphis and Charleston road with the Nashville and Chattanooga, with instructions to occupy Bridgeport also.

The enemy had meanwhile concentrated most of his forces at Chattanooga for the twofold purpose of holding this gateway of the Cumberland Mountains, and to assume a defensive attitude which would enable him to take advantage of such circumstances as might arise in the development of the offensive campaign he knew we must make. The peculiar topography of the country was much to his advantage, and while we had a broad river and numerous spurs and ridges of the Cumberland Mountains to cross at a long distance from our base, he was backed up on his depots of supply, and connected by interior lines of railway with the different armies of the Confederacy, so that he could be speedily reinforced.

Bridgeport was to be ultimately a sub-depot for storing subsistence supplies, and one of the points at which our army would cross the Tennessee, so I occupied it on July 29 with two brigades, retaining one at Stevenson, however, to protect that railway junction from raids by way of Caperton's ferry. By the 29th of August a considerable quantity of supplies had been accumulated, and then began a general movement of our troops for crossing the river. As there were not with the army enough pontoons to complete the two bridges required, I was expected to build one of them of trestles; and a battalion of the First Michigan Engineers under Colonel Innis was sent me to help construct the bridge. Early on the 3ist I sent into the neighboring woods about fifteen hundred men with axes and teams, and by nightfall they had delivered on the riverbank fifteen hundred logs suitable for a trestle bridge. Flooring had been shipped to me in advance by rail, but the quantity was insufficient, and the lack had to be supplied by utilizing planking and weatherboarding taken from barns and houses in the surrounding country. The next day Innis's engineers, with the assistance of the detail that had felled the timber, cut and half-notched the logs, and put the bridge across; spanning the main channel, which was swimming deep, with four or five pontoons that had been sent me for this purpose. On the 2d and 3d of September my division crossed on the bridge in safety, though we were delayed somewhat because of its giving way once where the pontoons joined the trestles. We were followed by a few detachments from other commands, and by nearly all the transportation of McCook's corps.

After getting to the south side of the Tennessee River I was ordered to Valley Head, where McCook's corps was to concentrate. On the 4th of September I ascended Sand Mountain, but had got only half way across the plateau, on top, when night came, the march having been a most toilsome one. The next day we descended to the base, and encamped near Trenton. On the 10th I arrived at Valley Head, and climbing Lookout Mountain, encamped on the plateau at Indian Falls. The following day I went down into Broomtown Valley to Alpine. The march of McCook's corps from Valley Head to Alpine was in pursuance of orders directing it to advance on Summerville, the possession of which place would further threaten the enemy's communications, it being assumed that Bragg was in full retreat south, as he had abandoned Chattanooga on the 8th. This assumption soon proved erroneous, however, and as we, while in Broomtown Valley, could not communicate directly with Thomas's corps, the scattered condition of the army began to alarm us all, and McCook abandoned the advance to Summerville, ordering back to the summit of Lookout Mountain such of the corps trains as had got down into Broomtown Valley.

But before this I had grown uneasy in regard to the disjointed situation of our army, and, to inform myself of what was going on, determined to send a spy into the enemy's lines. In passing Valley Head on the 10th my scout Card, who had been on the lookout for some one capable to undertake the task, brought me a Union man with whom he was acquainted, who lived on Sand Mountain, and had been much persecuted by guerrillas on account of his loyal sentiments. He knew the country well, and as his loyalty was vouched for I asked him to go into the enemy's camp, which I believed to be near Lafayette, and, bring me such information as he could gather. He said such a journey would be at the risk of his life, and that at best he could not expect to remain in that section of country if he undertook it, but that he would run all the chances if I would enable him to emigrate to the West at the end c f the "job," which I could do by purchasing the small "bunch" of stock he owned on the mountain. To this I readily assented, and he started on the delicate undertaking. He penetrated the enemy's lines with little difficulty, but while prosecuting his search for information was suspected, and at once arrested and placed under guard. From this critical situation he escaped; however, making his way through the enemy's picket-line in the darkness by crawling on his belly and deceiving the sentinels by imitating the grunts of the half-wild, sand-colored hogs with which the country abounded. He succeeded in reaching Rosecrans's headquarters finally, and there gave the definite information that Bragg intended to fight, and that he expected to be reinforced by Longstreet.

By this time it was clear that Bragg had abandoned Chattanooga with the sole design of striking us in detail as we followed in pursuit; and to prevent his achieving this purpose orders came at 12 o'clock, midnight, for McCook to draw in toward Chattanooga. This could be done only by recrossing Lookout Mountain, the enemy's army at Lafayette now interposing between us and Thomas's corps. The retrograde march began at once. I moved back over the mountain on the 13th and 14th to Stevens's Mills, and on the 15th and 16th recrossed through Stevens's Gap, in the Lookout range, and encamped at its base in McLamore's cove. The march was made with all possible celerity, for the situation was critical and demanded every exertion. The ascent and descent of the mountains was extremely exhausting, the steep grades often rendering it necessary to drag up and let down by hand both the transportation and artillery. But at last we were in conjunction with the main army, and my division breathed easier.

On the 17th I remained in line of battle all day and night in front of McLamore's cove, the enemy making slight demonstrations against me from the direction of Lafayette. The main body of the army having bodily moved to the left meanwhile, I followed it on the 18th, encamping at Pond Spring. On the 19th I resumed the march to the left and went into line of battle at Crawfish Springs to cover our right and rear. Immediately after forming this line, I again became isolated by the general movement to the left, and in consequence was directed to advance and hold the ford of Chickamauga Creek at Lee and Gordon's Mills, thus coming into close communication with the balance of our forces. I moved into this position rapidly, being compelled, though, first to drive back the enemy's cavalry skirmishers, who, having crossed to the west side of the creek, annoyed the right flank of my column a good deal while en route.

Upon arrival at Lee and Gordon's Mills I found the ford over Chickamauga Creek temporarily uncovered, through the hurried movement of Wood to the assistance of Davis's division. The enemy was already present in small force, with the evident intention of taking permanent possession, but my troops at once actively engaged him and recovered the ford with some slight losses. Scarcely had this been done when I was directed to assist Crittenden. Leaving Lytle's brigade at the ford, I proceeded with Bradley's and Laiboldt's to help Crittenden, whose main line was formed to the east of the Chattanooga and Lafayette road, its right trending toward a point on Chickamauga Creek about a mile and a half north of Lee and Gordon's Mills. By the time I had joined Crittenden with my two brigades, Davis had been worsted in an attack Rosecrans had ordered him to make on the left of that portion of the enemy's line which was located along the west bank of the Chickamauga, the repulse being so severe that one of Davis's batteries had to be abandoned. Bradley's brigade arrived on the ground first and was hastily formed and thrown into the fight, which up to this moment had been very doubtful, fortune inclining first to one side, then to the other. Bradley's brigade went in with steadiness, and charging across an open corn-field that lay in front of the Lafayette road, recovered Davis's guns and forced the enemy to retire. Meanwhile Laiboldt's brigade had come on the scene, and forming it on Bradley's right, I found myself at the end of the contest holding the ground which was Davis's original position. It was an ugly fight and my loss was heavy, including Bradley wounded. The temporary success was cheering, and when Lytle's brigade joined me a little later I suggested to Crittenden that we attack, but investigation showed that his troops, having been engaged all day, were not in condition, so the suggestion could not be carried out.

The events of the day had indicated that Bragg's main object was to turn Rosecrans's left; it was therefore still deemed necessary that the army should continue its flank movement to the left, so orders came to draw my troops in toward the widow Glenn's house. By strengthening the skirmish line and shifting my brigades in succession from right to left until the point designated was reached, I was able to effect the withdrawal without much difficulty, calling in my skirmish line after the main force had retired.

My command having settled down for the night in this new line I rode to army headquarters, to learn if possible the expectations for the morrow and hear the result of the battle in General Thomas's front. Nearly all the superior officers of the army were at headquarters, and it struck me that much depression prevailed, notwithstanding the fact that the enemy's attempts during the day to turn our left flank and also envelop our right had been unsuccessful. It was now positively known, through prisoners and otherwise, that Bragg had been reinforced to such an extent as to make him materially outnumber us, consequently there was much apprehension for the future.

The necessity of protecting our left was most apparent, and the next day the drifting in that direction was to be continued. This movement in the presence of the enemy, who at all points was actively seeking an opportunity to penetrate our line and interpose a column between its right and left, was most dangerous. But the necessity for shifting the army to the left was obvious, hence only the method by which it was undertaken is open to question. The move was made by the flank in the face of an exultant foe superior in numbers, and was a violation of a simple and fundamental military principle. Under such circumstances columns naturally stretch out into attenuated lines, organizations become separated, and intervals occur, all of which we experienced; and had the orders for the movement been construed properly I doubt if it could have been executed without serious danger. Necessity knows no law, however, and when all the circumstances of this battle are fully considered it is possible that justification may be found for the manoeuvres by which the army was thus drifted to the left. We were in a bad strait unquestionably, and under such conditions possibly the exception had to be applied rather than the rule.

At daylight on the morning of the 20th a dense fog obscured everything; consequently both armies were passive so far as fighting was concerned. Rosecrans took advantage of the inaction to rearrange his right, and I was pulled back closer to the widow Glenn's house to a strong position, where I threw together some rails and logs as barricades, but I was disconnected from the troops on my left by a considerable interval. Here I awaited the approach of the enemy, but he did not disturb me, although about 9 o'clock in the forenoon he had opened on our extreme left with musketry fire and a heavy cannonade. Two hours later it was discovered by McCook that the interval between the main army and me was widening, and he ordered me to send Laiboldt's brigade to occupy a portion of the front that had been covered by Negley's division. Before getting this brigade into place, however, two small brigades of Davis's division occupied the ground, and I directed Laiboldt to form in column of regiments on the crest of a low ridge in rear of Carlin's brigade, so as to prevent Davis's right flank from being turned. The enemy was now feeling Davis strongly, and I was about sending for Lytle's and Bradley's brigades when I received an order to move these rapidly to the, extreme left of the army to the assistance of General Thomas. I rode hastily back toward their position, but in the meanwhile, they had been notified by direct orders from McCook, and were moving out at a double-quick toward the Lafayette road. By this time the enemy had assaulted Davis furiously in front and flank, and driven him from his line, and as the confused mass came back, McCook ordered Laiboldt to charge by deploying to the front. This he did through Davis's broken ranks, but failed to check the enemy's heavy lines, and finally Laiboldt's brigade broke also and fell to the rear. My remaining troops, headed by Lytle, were now passing along the rear of the ground where this disaster took place — in column on the road — en route to Thomas, and as the hundreds of fugitives rushed back, McCook directed me to throw in Lytle's and Bradley's brigades. This was hastily done, they being formed to the front under a terrible fire. Scarcely were they aligned when the same horde of Confederates that had overwhelmed Davis and Laiboldt poured in upon them a deadly fire and shivered the two brigades to pieces. We succeeded in rallying them, however, and by a counter attack regained the ridge that Laiboldt had been driven from, where we captured the colors of the Twenty-fourth Alabama. We could not hold the ridge, though, and my troops were driven back with heavy loss, including General Lytle killed, past the widow Glenn's house, and till I managed to establish them in line of battle on a range of low hills behind the Dry Valley road.

During these occurrences General Rosecrans passed down the road behind my line, and sent word that he wished to see me, but affairs were too critical to admit of my going to him at once, and he rode on to Chattanooga. It is to be regretted that he did not wait till I could join him, for the delay would have permitted him to see that matters were not in quite such bad shape as he supposed; still, there is no disguising the fact that at this juncture his army was badly crippled.

Shortly after my division had rallied on the low hills already described, I discovered that the enemy, instead of attacking me in front, was wedging in between my division and the balance of the army; in short, endeavoring to cut me off from Chattanooga. This necessitated another retrograde movement, which brought me back to the southern face of Missionary Ridge, where I was joined by Carlin's brigade of Davis's division. Still thinking I could join General Thomas, I rode some distance to the left of my line to look for a way out, but found that the enemy had intervened so far as to isolate me effectually. I then determined to march directly to Rossville, and from there effect a junction with Thomas by the Lafayette road.

I reached Rossville about o'clock in the afternoon, bringing with me eight guns, forty-six caissons, and a long ammunition train, the latter having been found in a state of confusion behind the widow Glenn's when I was being driven back behind the Dry Valley road.

The head of my column passed through Rossville, appearing upon Thomas's left about 6 o'clock in the evening, penetrated without any opposition the right of the enemy's line, and captured several of his field-hospitals. As soon as I got on the field I informed Thomas of the presence of my command, and asked for orders. He replied that his lines were disorganized, and that it would be futile to attack; that all I could do was to hold on, and aid in covering his withdrawal to Rossville.

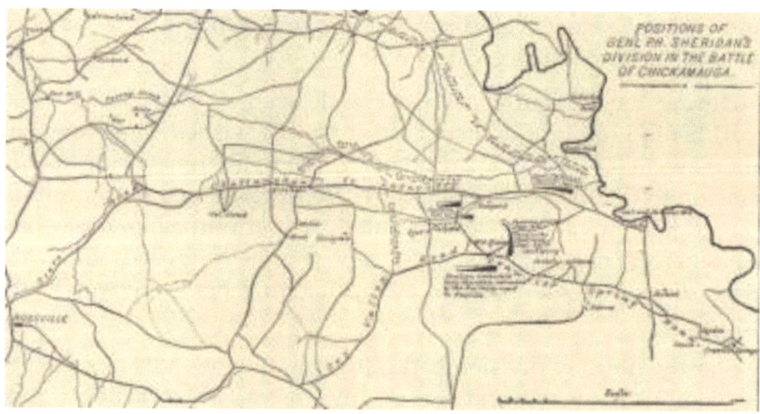

Enlarge

I accompanied him back to Rossville, and when we reached the skirt of the little hamlet General Thomas halted and we dismounted. Going into one of the angles of a worm fence near by I took a rail from the top and put it through the lower rails at a proper height

100

from the ground to make a seat, and General Thomas and I sat down while, my troops were moving by. The General appeared very much exhausted, seemed to forget what he had stopped for, and said little or nothing of the incidents of the day. This was the second occasion on which I had met him in the midst of misfortune, for during the fight in the cedars at Stone River, when our prospects were most disheartening, we held a brief conversation respecting the line he was then taking up for the purpose of helping me. At other times, in periods of inactivity, I saw but little of him. He impressed me, now as he did in the cedars, his quiet, unobtrusive: demeanor communicating a gloomy rather than a hopeful view of the situation. This apparent depression was due no doubt to the severe trial through which he had gone in the last forty-eight hours, which, strain had exhausted him very much both physically and mentally. His success in maintaining his ground was undoubtedly largely influenced by the fact that two-thirds of the National forces had been sent to his succor, but his firm purpose to save the army was the mainstay on which all relied after Rosecrans left the field. As the command was getting pretty well past, I rose to go in order to put my troops into camp. This aroused the General, when, remarking that he had a little flask of brandy in his saddle-holster, he added that he had just stopped for the purpose of offering me a drink, as he knew I must be very tired. He requested one of his staff-officers to get the flask, and after taking a sip himself, passed it to me. Refreshed by the brandy, I mounted and rode off to supervise the encamping of my division, by no means an easy task considering the darkness, and the confusion that existed among the troops that had preceded us into Rossville.

This done, I lay down at the foot of a tree, with my saddle for a pillow, and saddle-blanket for a cover. Some soldiers near me having built a fire, were making coffee, and I guess I must have been looking on wistfully, for in a little while they brought me a tin-cupful of the coffee and a small piece of hard bread, which I relished keenly, it being the first food that had passed my lips since the night before. I was very tired, very hungry, and much discouraged by what had taken place since morning. I had been obliged to fight my command under the most disadvantageous circumstances, disconnected, without supports, without even opportunity to form in line of battle, and at one time contending against four divisions of the enemy. In this battle of Chickamauga, out of an effective strength Of 4,000 bayonets, I had lost 1,517 officers and men, including two brigade commanders. This was not satisfactory indeed, it was most depressing—and then there was much confusion prevailing around Rossville; and, this condition of things doubtless increasing my gloomy reflections, it did not seem to me that the outlook for the next day was at all auspicious, unless the enemy was slow to improve his present advantage. Exhaustion soon quieted all forebodings, though, and I fell into a sound sleep, from which I was not aroused till daylight.

On the morning of the 21st the enemy failed to advance, and his inaction gave us the opportunity for getting the broken and disorganized army into shape. It took a large part of the day to accomplish this, and the chances of complete victory would have been greatly in Bragg's favor if he could have attacked us vigorously at this time. But he had been badly hurt in the two days' conflict, and his inactivity on the 21st showed that he too had to go through the process of reorganization. Indeed, his crippled condition began to show itself the preceding evening, and I have always thought that, had General Thomas held on and attacked the Confederate right and rear from where I made the junction with him on the Lafayette road, the field of Chickamauga would have been relinquished to us; but it was fated to be otherwise.

Rosecrans, McCook, and Crittenden passed out of the battle when they went back to Chattanooga, and their absence was discouraging to all aware of it. Doubtless this had much to do with Thomas's final withdrawal, thus leaving the field to the enemy, though at an immense cost in killed and wounded. The night of the 21st the army moved back from Rossville, and my division, as the rearguard of the Twentieth Corps, got within our lines at Chattanooga about 8 o'clock the morning of the 22d. Our unmolested retirement from Rossville lent additional force to the belief that the enemy had been badly injured, and further impressed me with the conviction that we might have held on. Indeed, the battle of Chickamauga was somewhat like that of Stone River, victory resting with the side that had the grit to defer longest its relinquishment of the field.

The manoeuvres by which Rosecrans had carried his army over the Cumberland Mountains, crossed the Tennessee River, and possessed himself of Chattanooga, merit the highest commendation up to the abandonment of this town by Bragg on the 8th of September; but I have always fancied that that evacuation made Rosecrans over-confident, and led him to think that he could force Bragg south as far as Rome. After the Union army passed the river and Chattanooga fell into our hands; we still kept pressing the enemy's communications, and the configuration of the country necessitated more or less isolation of the different corps. McCook's corps of three divisions had crossed two difficult ridges—Sand and Lookout mountains—to Alpine in Broomtown Valley with intentions against Summerville. Thomas's corps had marched by the way of Stevens's Gap toward Lafayette, which he expected to occupy. Crittenden had passed through Chattanooga, at first directing his march an Ringgold. Thus the corps of the army were not in conjunction, and between McCook and Thomas there intervened a positive and aggressive obstacle in the shape of Bragg's army concentrating and awaiting reinforcement at Lafayette. Under these circumstances Bragg could have taken the different corps in detail, and it is strange that he did not, even before receiving his reinforcements, turn on McCook in Broomtown Valley and destroy him.

Intelligence that Bragg would give battle began to come to us from various sources as early as the 10th of September, and on the 11th McCook found that he could not communicate with Thomas by the direct road through Broomtown Valley; but we did not begin closing in toward Chattanooga till the 13th, and even then the Twentieth Corps had before it the certainty of many delays that must necessarily result from the circuitous and difficult mountain roads which we would be obliged to follow. Had the different corps, beginning with McCook's, been drawn in toward Chattanooga between the 8th and 12th of September, the objective point of the campaign would have remained in our hands without the battle of Chickamauga, but, as has been seen, this was not done. McCook was almost constantly on the march day and night between the 13th and the 19th, ascending and descending mountains, his men worried and wearied, so that when they appeared on the battle-field, their fatigued condition operated greatly against their efficiency.

This delay in concentration was also the original cause of the continuous shifting toward our left to the support of Thomas, by which manoeuvre Rosecrans endeavored to protect his communications with Chattanooga, and out of which grew the intervals that offered such tempting opportunities to Bragg. In addition to all this, much transpired on the field of battle tending to bring about disaster. There did not seem to be any well-defined plan of action in the fighting; and this led to much independence of judgment in construing orders among some of the subordinate generals. It also gave rise to much license in issuing orders: too many people were giving important directions, affecting the whole army, without authority from its head. In view, therefore, of all the errors that were committed from the time Chattanooga fell into our hands after our first crossing the Tennessee, it was fortunate that the Union defeat was not more complete, that it left in the enemy's possession not much more than the barren results arising from the simple holding of the ground on which the engagement was fought.